Quebec SILVER

from the Collection of the National Gallery of Canada

Quebec
SILVER

from the Collection of
the National Gallery of Canada

RENÉ VILLENEUVE

NATIONAL GALLERY OF CANADA
OTTAWA 1998

Produced by the Publications Division of
the National Gallery of Canada, Ottawa.
Chief: Serge Thériault
Editors: Susan McMaster, Myriam Afriat,
Jacques Pichette
Picture Editor: Colleen Evans

Translation by Bob Sandler, Montreal.
Designed and typeset by Associés libres, Montreal.
Typeset in Caslon 540.
Printed on Potlatch Mountie Matte Recycled.
Film by Grafix Studio, Montreal.
Printed by The Lowe-Martin Group.

The concurrent exhibition *Quebec Silver from the
Collection of the National Gallery of Canada*, organized
and circulated by the National Gallery, presents a
selection of works from the permanent collection.

Itinerary

Art Gallery of Greater Victoria
10 July – 14 September 1997

Winnipeg Art Gallery
10 October 1997 – 4 January 1998

the Gallery/Stratford
1 June – 13 September 1998

Musée du Québec, Quebec City
17 February – 1 May 1999

Lowe Art Museum, University of Miami, Coral Gables
2 December 1999 – 23 January 2000

Canadian Cataloguing in Publication Data

National Gallery of Canada.
Quebec silver from the collection of the National
Gallery of Canada.

Issued also in French under title: Orfèvrerie québécoise
de la collection du Musée des beaux-arts du Canada.
Includes bibliographical references: p.
Includes index.
ISBN 0-88884-659-2

1. Silverwork–Quebec (Province). 2. National Gallery
of Canada–Catalogs. I. Villeneuve, René, 1960– .
II. Title.

NK7113 A3 Q83 1998
739.2'37714'074471384   C98-986001-9

Photograph Credits

Photographs for figures have been provided
by the owners or custodians of the works
reproduced, except for the following:

Archives nationales du Québec, Quebec City 3
McGill University, Montreal, Ramsay Traquair Fonds 6
National Gallery of Canada, Ottawa 24, 36, 48
National Gallery of Canada archives, Ottawa 1, 26
University of King's College, Halifax 2

Available through your local bookseller or through The
Bookstore, National Gallery of Canada, 380 Sussex Drive,
P.O. Box 427, Station A, Ottawa, Ontario K1N 9N4.

Front and Back Covers

Laurent Amiot
Coffee Pot from the Le Moine Family c. 1796
(see fig. 35)

CONTENTS

FOREWORD

The National Gallery's acquisitions took a new turn in the 1920s, thanks to Marius Barbeau, an ethnologist at the neighbouring National Museum of Man. Actively involved with traditional Quebec arts and crafts, Barbeau initiated the first acquisitions for the collection today identified as Early Canadian Art, including a pair of anonymous statuettes portraying the *Virgin* and *Christ* purchased in 1928, a set of arrow sashes, and a fine selection of woven items from Charlevoix county in Quebec.

Two curators who arrived at the Gallery after the Second World War, Robert Hubbard and Russell Harper, shared this interest in early Quebec art, and enlarged the collection considerably. Their efforts led to the donation by E.E. Poole in 1962 of the *Immaculate Conception* by Salomon Marion – the only silver statue known to be made in Canada and the first piece of Quebec silver acquired. This generous gift paved the way for the purchase of eight more pieces of liturgical silver in 1965.

In 1971, Jean Trudel was appointed as the first Curator of Early Canadian Art. The exhibition *Silver in New France*, which he mounted in 1974, confirmed the Gallery's commitment to the art of silverwork. Five years later a significant expansion of the holdings occurred when the firm of Henry Birks and Sons donated its imposing collection to the Gallery, comprising more than seven thousand pieces of silver amassed between 1936 and 1979, most of them from Quebec. Of these, many were on deposit at other Canadian museums, placed there by the collector to make them more widely accessible – a system which the Gallery maintained. With the arrival of curator Ross Fox in 1980, official cataloguing began, leading to the exhibition *Presentation Pieces and Trophies from the Henry Birks Collection of Canadian Silver*, shown across Canada in 1984 and 1985. The accompanying catalogue has become a standard reference.

The National Gallery moved into its new building in 1988, allowing René Villeneuve, the current Assistant Curator of Early Canadian Art, to exhibit silver alongside contemporary painting and sculpture for the first time. In following years, he has re-evaluated the original deposits of silverwork at other museums and harmonized them with their host collections.

The broad-ranging research and original analysis presented in this publication by René Villeneuve offer a fresh, new look at an essential part of our artistic heritage. A concurrent exhibition selected from the best works in the collection travels across Canada and internationally until the year 2000.

PIERRE THÉBERGE, C.Q.
Director
National Gallery of Canada

PREFACE AND ACKNOWLEDGMENTS

The publication of a book that would foster an appreciation of the National Gallery's collection of Canadian silver was proposed more than a decade ago, in 1987, when the layout of the present building and reinstallation of the collections were being planned. The suggestion met with immediate enthusiasm. We were all convinced of the need to draw greater attention to this immense body of works, one that was well known in general terms but whose scope and outstanding quality remained, for the most part, undiscovered.

The project was spurred on by some additional considerations. To begin with, it seemed appropriate to introduce a public largely unaware of this aspect to the work carried out by Henry Gifford Birks in amassing the core of the collection. In the larger context, there was and still is a dearth of studies on Canadian silver of all periods. Among those that exist, a number deal with the intricate matter of marks used by silversmiths and manufacturers and provide biographical accounts of the artists – approaches not to be disparaged by any means – but little has been written to promote an understanding of the intrinsic qualities of the objects themselves. This last aspect seemed the more relevant in that the proposed volume was intended primarily, although not exclusively, for visitors to the National Gallery and to the exhibitions of the collection which travel from time to time across Canada and internationally.

At an overall level, therefore, it became clear that the aim of this study should not be so much to present new information as to cast a brighter light on the field of silversmithing, which lies in a grey area of current art history. Emphasis has thus been placed on two distinct but subtly related features of the collection: how it was formed, and how it may be appreciated within the larger realm of art. The first chapter focusses attention on the manner in which the collection was gathered, beginning with Henry G. Birks himself, his purposes, his choices and their implications, and the historical context in which he operated. This endeavour opens up a rich and dynamic world, and in turn defines the object of study for the second chapter. Here, the discussion expands to include other works held by the National Gallery, which has continued to acquire selected pieces in the same spirit that guided Birks's quest. As well, it examines some rare items from collections held elsewhere – a widening of focus that Birks, with his great passion for silver, would surely have approved for the insights it yields. The result is a selective analysis of an enormous and highly varied body of work. Grown far beyond the original aim of providing a detailed history of the development of the silversmith's craft in Quebec, the chapter focusses on specific works to explore the major stages in the stylistic evolution of Quebec silver from the seventeenth to the twentieth centuries. It concludes by highlighting the originality of the silver produced in this place and period of North American history.

The investigation of documentary sources, essential to the success of the undertaking, led me down various paths. I profited from the support and expertise of colleagues at other institutions, as well as archivists and librarians, all of whom were unstinting in their efforts to assist me. Among those based in Canada, I am profoundly indebted to Howard Collinson and Peter Kaellgren of the Royal Ontario Museum in Toronto and to the staff at the Thomas Fisher Rare Book Library of the University of Toronto; in Quebec City, to Danièle Rompré at the Musée de la Civilisation, Nicole Perron at the Musée de l'Hôtel-Dieu, and Armand Gagné at the Archdiocese of Quebec; and in Montreal, to Rosalind Pepall at the Montreal Museum of Fine Arts, Virginia Watts at the Canadian Guild of Crafts, and Françoise Roux, formerly at the Blackader-Lauterman Library of McGill University.

My research required that I turn to colleagues outside Canada, and I wish to express my deep gratitude to David Barquist at the Yale University Art Gallery, Clare LeCorbelier at The Metropolitan Museum in New York, Donald L. Fennimore at the Henry Francis du Pont Winterthur Museum in Delaware, James W. Tottis at The Detroit Institute of Arts, Judy Throm at the Archives of American Art in Washington, D.C., and Daniel Alcouffe at the Musée du Louvre and Catherine Arminjon at the Inventaire général, both in Paris.

For their co-operation, I most heartily thank the dealers Bert Baron, Arthur G. Bousquet, and Wynyard R.T. Wilkinson, who generously agreed to impart their valuable knowledge. I should also like to pay tribute to John L. Russell, who freely shared his insights, enabling me to better grasp the dynamics of the Canadian art and antique markets during the last half century. My warm thanks go as well to those collectors who have chosen to remain anonymous.

I also wish to extend my deepest appreciation to those closer at hand who have contributed to this project on a daily basis, in particular Claire Berthiaume, who performed her secretarial duties with unwavering constancy, John B. Collins and Jean-Pierre Labiau, who successively assisted me with extraordinary rigour and professionalism, and the staff of the Publications Division, including Serge Thériault, Myriam Afriat, Susan McMaster, Jacques Pichette, and Colleen Evans. Together with the staff from Photography, they made it possible to produce this elegant volume.

I am profoundly grateful as well to Russell Armstrong, Andrew Jones, and Claude Thibault for their understanding and support throughout these months devoted to studying the silver collection.

Finally, I would like to thank Charles C. Hill, Curator of Canadian Art, for the unfailing confidence he has shown in me during the realization of this project.

RENÉ VILLENEUVE

Fig. 1
Henry Gifford Birks giving a speech on silver
for the opening of an exhibition of works
selected from the *Henry Birks Collection of
Canadian Silver* at the Maison Del Vecchio
in Montreal in 1970.

Henry G. Birks
His Story and His Collection

by Virginia B. Alexandor

Henry Gifford Birks was a successful businessman, active in his community, valued by his family, with a wide circle of friends. He also had a singular passion.

That passion has since been transformed into a tangible gift to all Canadians. He has presented us with a superb collection of early Canadian silver, a unique illustration of the artistry and ingenuity of our early silversmiths. He was one of the first to recognise the richness of this aspect of our cultural heritage.

Born in 1892, the eldest son of William Massey Birks and Miriam Childs Gifford, Henry and his family lived on Stanley Street just north of Sherbrooke in Montreal. Like his six siblings, he became fluent in French at an early age, speaking it more naturally than English for a time.

One of Henry's first memories was of visiting the Henry Birks store as a boy of six: he was knocked to the floor by a swinging gate that closed off the area behind the counters. Undeterred, he returned to work as a messenger during summer and Christmas holidays, and entered formal employment in 1911 at the age of seventeen. When the First World War broke out in August 1914, Henry immediately enlisted with the forty-second battalion of the Black Watch Regiment. Badly wounded in France, he was invalided home in 1916, and took a number of years to fully regain his robust health. Despite this, he became secretary-treasurer of the company in 1917. For a few years he shared a "partners" or double desk with his grandfather, Henry. The elder man died in 1928, and his namesake went on to become general manager in 1933 and president in 1944.

In June 1917, Henry married Lilian Cockshutt Drummond, daughter of George Drummond and niece of the poet William Henry Drummond. George Drummond had built a home in the old Seigneury of Montarville, now Saint-Bruno, twenty miles east of Montreal. The Birks followed suit in 1920, building their home above Mill Lake overlooking Lac Seigneurial. Their friend Marius Barbeau, the noted ethnologist, was invited to help choose a name, and suggested "Nontarakay," a Huron-Wyandot word meaning "between the lakes." Nontarakay was to remain the focal point for Henry and his family during summers and weekends throughout his career.

With its mountain, orchards, and lakes, it was an idyllic, peaceful, place, within easy distance of the city. The Seigneury of Saint-Bruno later became a syndicate owned by the Drummond, Birks, and Pease families. (Edson Loy Pease was a banker with the Royal Bank in the first decades of the century; he heard about the property in Saint-Bruno through his work.) Henry's children, George Drummond, Sheila Gifford, and Willa Kathleen grew up there. Henry was fond of saying, "I exist in the city but I live in the country." The Old Mill in Saint-Bruno was the centre for family gatherings – costume parties, charades, corn roasts, plays – and Sunday Evensong, with family members reading the lessons and playing the foot-pedal organ. As Henry and Lilian's niece, I often participated in these occasions and remember them fondly. The mill became the site of fourteen marriages and twenty-three baptisms. Today it is a small museum, and the grounds beyond the private residential properties are maintained by the Quebec Government as a public park.

Around 1935, Birks became aware that a lot of early Canadian silver was disappearing. Old pieces were being melted down and recast in a new style; others were being traded in as down payments on new pieces – a custom common in Europe. The stock-market crash in 1929 and the Depression that followed also led to a dearth of early Canadian silver because many parish priests were obliged to sell pieces just to maintain their churches.

Birks's curiosity about the field was first expressed through a search for early pieces made by the Hendery and Leslie firm. Because there was no guild or assay office in Canada, silversmiths used a personal mark or left their work unmarked. Retailers often added their own stamp to pieces, which might or might not have the maker's name or initials on them. He began his search by compiling his own list of the marks used by Hendery and Leslie. The list soon expanded to include marks of makers in Montreal, Quebec City, and Trois Rivières, and later Nova Scotia and Ontario.

As he deepened his research, Henry began collecting the pieces which came his way, displaying them in a glass case in his office until it became too small. The collection grew, and Henry became an enthusiastic student of old silver, seeking out expert advice. The well known antique dealer and appraiser Harry M. Allice began to bring him pieces of silver in the 1950s, and also to introduce him to other dealers. Allice had been a close friend of the collector Louis Carrier, a man twenty years his senior, who had been director of the Chateau Ramezay in Montreal as well as author of a number of articles on the subject. Allice eventually replaced Carrier as *the* silver expert in Montreal. He became a great friend of Henry's and the two of them could spend several hours looking at one item together, holding it, admiring it, and discussing every detail of its manufacture, history, and marks.

By this time Henry had engaged excellent curators for the collection, first Helen (Elfie) Drummond, and then Thelma Graham. Harry often joined Henry, Helen, or Thelma for lunch in the boardroom to discuss old silver. He became the "question-mark man" whenever a maker or a mark was in doubt. People were constantly calling on Birks as well: every dealer knew he would be interested in buying any good piece. As far as the dealers were concerned, Henry G. Birks was "the King," according to Allice.

He did quite a bit of scouting for old silver on his own as well. Sometimes, while out for a drive with his wife and friends, he would stop and call on someone whom he had learned might have something interesting to sell. Even a relative, on showing him a piece of her own early silver, would hear the quick question, "Want to sell it?" When visiting the Henry Birks store in Quebec City, Henry often scheduled extra time to visit the dealers there.

Meanwhile, the business was flourishing under the management of Henry and two trusted employees, Ralph Johnson, who joined the company in 1919 and eventually became vice-president of finance, and Earle Gallagher, who started about the same time and became vice-president of merchandising. They worked together as a team for over forty years. He also had the dedicated assistance of his son, Drummond, who eventually took over, becoming senior operating officer in 1967 and president in 1972.

Birks also took an active part in civic and business affairs. He was on the Montreal City Council from 1941–44, and was president of both the Montreal Board of Trade and the Canadian Chamber of Commerce, a governor of McGill University, president of the Building Owners and Managers Association, chair of the Montreal Theological Colleges, and director of at least seven companies.

He was also one of very few Canadians (along with his father and son) to become a freeman of the Worshipful Company of Goldsmiths in London, England. In 1967 he was presented with the Confederation Medal – the honour which preceded the Order of Canada – by the Queen.

Every year Henry crossed the country, visiting every Birks store. In the later years Lilian travelled with him, until they were in their mid-seventies. He made a point of remembering the name of every staff person, as well as details about their families and lives. While he spoke with the men in the store, Lilian would often invite the women for tea in the local hotel. He spent considerable vacation time writing postcards to staff members and often sent birthday cards as well. As his secretary of twenty-two years, Constance Gray, recalls: "He was an excellent boss – he always knew what he wanted …. He expected you to work hard, but he worked very hard himself. Anything he took up he did very thoroughly. He had an excellent memory. He was popular with the staff, who felt they were treated fairly."

Birks loved sharing his enthusiasm for Canadian silver. He had one speech that covered the history of silver from the earliest known times, which he presented first at the National Museum of Man in Ottawa, and then on some forty other occasions. He enhanced it with slides showing how a silver teapot is made from start to finish. Occasionally, he took groups of school children through his own silver factory himself.

Henry Birks had an immense love for Canada. Every part of it was important to him. Above all, he held a special feeling for Quebec, the province where his forebears had settled and prospered. He had many opportunities to speak publicly, and one of his favourite themes was national unity.

In 1978, Henry Birks retired from the business; he died on 8 November 1985, in his ninety-fourth year. His collection of the early artistry of silversmiths in Canada took forty years of continuous search and study to assemble; it is the largest, most comprehensive, and best documented compilation of its kind. His wish to offer it as a gift to the whole nation was fulfilled through the donation of the Henry Birks Collection of Canadian Silver to the National Gallery of Canada in 1979. Henry G. Birks has given us the opportunity to see, learn about, and appreciate a generally overlooked area of our past. Silver is not only wonderful to use, it holds a special and worthy place among the beautiful objects of our Canadian cultural history.

GENESIS OF A COLLECTION

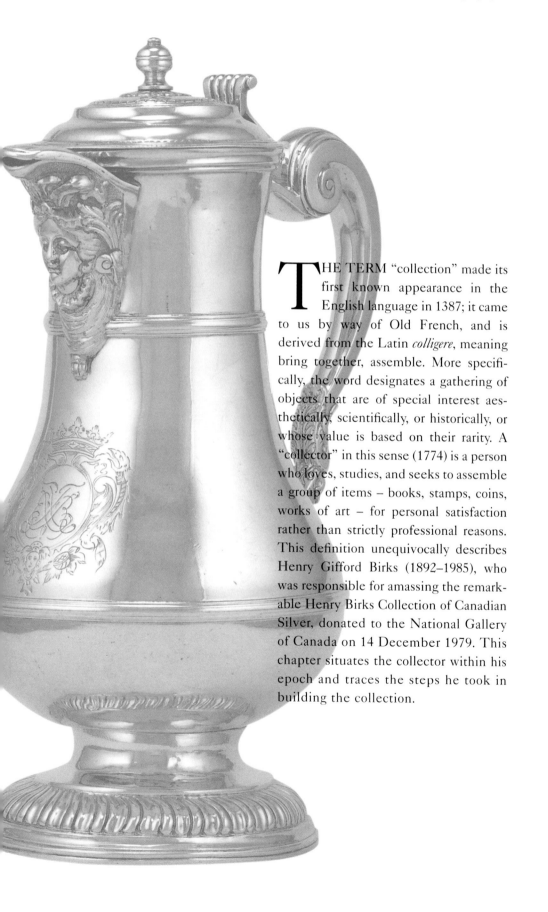

HE TERM "collection" made its first known appearance in the English language in 1387; it came to us by way of Old French, and is derived from the Latin *colligere*, meaning bring together, assemble. More specifically, the word designates a gathering of objects that are of special interest aesthetically, scientifically, or historically, or whose value is based on their rarity. A "collector" in this sense (1774) is a person who loves, studies, and seeks to assemble a group of items – books, stamps, coins, works of art – for personal satisfaction rather than strictly professional reasons. This definition unequivocally describes Henry Gifford Birks (1892–1985), who was responsible for amassing the remarkable Henry Birks Collection of Canadian Silver, donated to the National Gallery of Canada on 14 December 1979. This chapter situates the collector within his epoch and traces the steps he took in building the collection.

Fig. 2
Davenport Pottery
Longport, Staffordshire, England, c. 1793–1887
Wine Cooler c. 1800–15
Terra cotta
University of King's College, Halifax

This wine cooler belonged originally to Charles Ramage Prescott (1772–1859) of Starr's Point, Nova Scotia.

The Beginnings

The Birks collection was assembled in a context of growing national awareness in the New World. Just as the presentation of the famous "Colonial New England Kitchen" at the Brooklyn and Long Island Fair in 1864 signalled a rising sense of American national identity, which eventually led to the formation of collections devoted to Colonial decorative art, a similar consciousness was emerging in Canada as a result of Confederation in 1867, and private collections were also being created. One of the first was initiated in Halifax. On 18 May 1880, Judge John W. Weldon and his wife gave their collection of *Specimens of China Brought to the Colonies by the Early Settlers, Particularly the Loyalist* to the King's College Library (fig. 2). This collection, containing more than 300 pieces, was brought together by Mrs Weldon over a period of about fifteen years, probably between 1860 and 1875. She was considerably more concerned with the provenance of these porcelain and ceramic items than with their identification, noting: "It is hoped that it will be borne in mind that [the collection] must be valued not for its intrinsic worth, but as recollections of the early settlers in these colonies, among which will be found several contributions from families of later arrival."[1]

The Weldon initiative, exceptional for the period, foreshadowed an awakening of interest more properly associated with the first third of the twentieth century. Sigmund Samuel (1867–1962) of Toronto started to collect Canadian drawings, watercolours, books, and historical paintings before 1910, at a time when such works were thought to be of little value. In 1914, Samuel and his family moved to England, where he actively continued to enrich his collection throughout a twenty-five year stay. England was fertile hunting ground for enthusiasts interested in such works. Samuel returned to Toronto in 1939, and gave his collection to the Royal Ontario Museum in Toronto over the next four years, although he continued to acquire works until his death in 1962. Still housed in the ROM, the Samuel Collection, in the Canadiana Department, includes 1702 watercolours and drawings, 2000 engravings, some 150 paintings, and approximately 200 rare books.[2]

Similarly, William Hugh Coverdale (1871–1949) amassed his own group of early watercolours, engravings, maps, and oil paintings, selecting works that represented Canada's rich history. Coverdale did not start building his collection until 1928–29, several years after Samuel began his.[3] When purchased by the Canadian government in 1971, the Manoir Richelieu Collection included 2482 works, some of which were transferred to the National Archives of Canada (then the Public Archives of Canada).[4] Some were passed on to the National Gallery. The paintings remain with the Power Corporation in Montreal.

Coverdale also developed an interest in the furniture of rural Quebec. Although he was the president and general manager of Canada Steamship Lines from 1922 until 1949, his main residence was in New York, and he may have been influenced by similar American initiatives. At the very least, he must have drawn inspiration from the 1924 opening of the American Wing at the Metropolitan Museum of Art. There was certainly no shortage of such undertakings in the United States at the time. Coverdale's collection was originally assembled to furnish the second Hôtel Tadoussac, built in 1942; he assigned May Cole the task of outfitting the hotel with items of Canadiana.[5] Given the nature of the venture, she probably had to gather the pieces together within a relatively short period of time. No further additions appear to have been made to the collection after Coverdale's death in 1949. By the end of 1942, it included not only furniture, but copper, pewter, and earthenware as well. It was exhibited at the Musée de la province de Québec (since 1964, the Musée du Québec), from December 1942 until January 1943, and proved to be quite a revelation for many viewers.[6] Most of the furniture, approximately 250 pieces, was supplied by the Montreal antique dealer Samuel Breitman. The bulk of the furniture was acquired by the Quebec government in 1968. Originally deposited at the Musée du Québec, it is now housed at the Musée de la Civilisation, also in Quebec City.[7]

The growing enthusiasm for the vernacular is further evidenced by the existence of the collection of early Quebec sculpture assembled by Paul Gouin (1898–1976), a man whose activities and achievements have yet to be studied in depth. Although the precise moment he began collecting has not been established, he was well launched by the early 1940s. Gouin's interest may have sprung from his involvement in reopening the museum of rural arts and crafts at the school of furniture-making – the Musée des arts et métiers du terroir, École du Meuble – after the fire of 1 June 1940, for he deposited his collection in the building that was to become the new museum.[8] Gérard Morisset photographed it in this location in 1943.[9] In 1951, approximately 350 pieces were acquired by the Musée de la province de Québec at the instigation of Morisset himself.[10]

Each of these collections grew out of an interest in a particular field – porcelain, watercolour and engraving, furniture, or sculpture. Despite their differing orientations, however, they may all be viewed as part of a general effort to define a specifically national identity. Moreover, the fact that all of them were ultimately entrusted to public institutions not only attests to the confidence placed in these organizations, but also to a common desire to define the character of the young nation. The Henry Birks Collection of Canadian Silver appears to be a manifestation of this same trend. Before examining it in detail, however, we must first situate it within another context – that of other silver collections.

Nineteenth-century Collectors

Collectors began to show an interest in Quebec silver in the nineteenth century. Joseph Signaÿ (1778–1850), the first archbishop of Quebec, could perhaps be considered as the first collector of Quebec silver?[11] There can be no doubt that he had a marked interest in the field, leading him to assemble a great variety of silver

Fig. 3
Already by the end of the nineteenth century, Quebec City boasted a significant group of collectors and historians. This photograph was taken in front of Spencer Grange, the country home on the estate of James MacPherson Le Moine. From left to right: G.M. Fairchild, Cyrille Tessier, John Budden, James MacPherson Le Moine, Jennie Le Moine, Quiennie Fairchild, Alex Ferguson, and Robert J. Wickenden.

objects, now held by the Quebec archdiocese. In addition to numerous items of flatware, often bearing Signaÿ's monogram, this collection includes important pieces whose high quality and diverse origins suggest that the archbishop chose them with great care. The most remarkable are undoubtedly the Parisian *Ewer* by Éloi Guérin (c. 1714–1765), the *Ecuelle* (bowl with two flat handles), also Parisian, by Claude-Antoine Charivet (before 1740–1782), the late-eighteenth-century *Coffee Pot* by an unknown Londoner, the *Ewer* by Laurent Amiot (1764–1839), and the *Tea Tray* and *Cake Basket* by Salomon Marion (1782–1830), all of which are exceptional within the context of contemporary Quebec. The bishop's interest in silver is confirmed by the testament he dictated on 14 December 1841, in which he carefully described "a large silver chalice from the workshop of the late M. Laurent Amiot, and its paten," and gave instructions on the disposition of the silver tableware.[12] He also paid great attention to church treasures during his pastoral visits, often leaving specific directives regarding their maintenance and repair, and even the acquisition of particular pieces, especially sacred vessels.[13] In his conscientiousness and his enthusiasm, Signaÿ was the prototype for a long line of collectors.

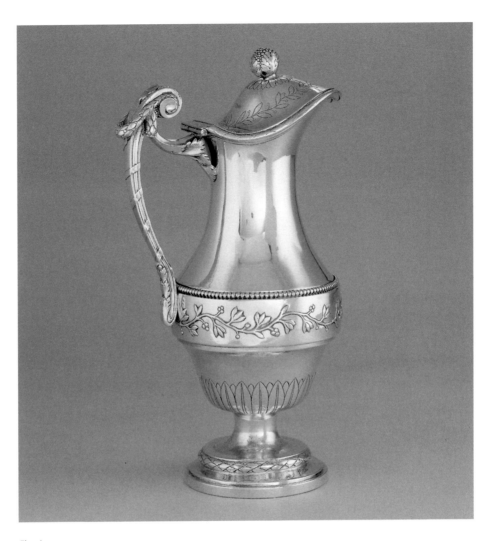

Fig. 4
Laurent Amiot
Quebec City 1764–1839
Ewer c. 1790
Silver
NGC, Gift of the Henry Birks Collection of Canadian Silver, 1979 (24008)

Another prominent resident of Quebec City who assembled various collections was the notary Cyrille Tessier (1835–1931).[14] Unfortunately, since research into Canadian collectors is still in its infancy, Tessier is yet another figure whose achievements have been largely ignored. In company with others of similar interests (fig. 3), he studied ancient objects, then referred to as "antiquities," and their historical context. His coins, medals, and books were eventually moved to the Séminaire de Québec. Tessier also had a consuming interest in early silver. According to family lore, the notary occasionally accepted articles of silver as payment, especially

Fig. 5
Laurent Amiot
Quebec City 1764–1839
Sauce Tureen c. 1825
Silver
NGC, Gift of the Henry Birks Collection of Canadian Silver, 1979 (24096.1–2)

when settling estates. We have not been able to find a complete list of the contents of his collection, which has since been broken up. We have been able to establish that he owned a number of superb items, including a large *Ewer* (fig. 4) and *Sauce Tureen* (fig. 5) by Amiot, both now at the National Gallery of Canada. He also owned several pieces currently at the Musée du Québec: two Parisian *Plates*, one by Michel Delapierre (before 1737–after 1785) and the other by Nicolas-Clément Vallières (who was accredited by the French guild as "Maître," or master silversmith, in 1732), a *Tea Caddy* by Charles Aldridge (1758–?, accredited 1775), a *Coffee Pot* and *Teapot* bearing the mark of Robert Hennell (1741–1811) and David Hennell (1767–?; Robert and David were partners, active 1795–1802), a *Tea Urn* by John Scofield (accredited before 1776), an *Armband* by William Bateman (1774–1850), a small *Ewer* by Amiot, and an *Indian Chief's Headdress* by Joseph Tison (1785–1869).[15] A member of the first generation of silver enthusiasts, Tessier assembled a remarkable group of pieces, chosen for their aesthetic and historic qualities, with no great concern for their place of manufacture.

Given Tessier's associations with various religious institutions, he quite possibly met the authority E. Alfred Jones (1872–1943) during Jones's visit to Quebec City in 1912, when he was being guided around the city by the Abbé Lionel Saint-George Lindsay. British in origin, Jones made a important contribution to the development and diffusion of knowledge of English silver in the first half of this century. He was especially interested in religious items, as well as in the royal collections of England and Russia. Also to his credit are the publication of beautiful editions cataloguing the collections held by the principal colleges of Oxford and Cambridge universities. He became interested in Quebec silver while heading a project on colonial American silver, a project which resulted in a luxurious catalogue published in 1913.[16]

The Twentieth Century

It is impossible to discuss early Quebec silver without mentioning Ramsay H. Traquair (1874–1952). Of Scottish origin, Traquair arrived in Canada in 1913. That same year, he became a professor of architecture at McGill University, and in 1914 succeeded Percy Nobbs as MacDonald Professor of Architecture. In addition to pursuing his professional goals, he was very much involved in Montreal cultural circles. He became a member of the Arts Club in Montreal right away, and in 1917 joined the Pen and Pencil Club. Between 1918 and 1925, he served on the board of the Canadian Guild of Crafts, then the Canadian Handicrafts Guild,[17] but he became actively interested in Quebec silver only from about 1928 to 1940 (fig. 6).[18] When visiting churches and long-established religious communities during summer excursions, he sometimes documented the items they owned. He also visited private collectors and the descendants of old Quebec families. In addition to photographing the pieces themselves, he frequently sketched their marks, and several times made rubbings. Few of Traquair's own field notes appear to have survived, but we know he referred to transcripts provided by Marius Barbeau, Gordon Nielson, and Édouard-Zotique Massicotte, to name the most important. His research culminated in the publication of *The Old Silver of Quebec* in 1940, under the auspices of the Art Association of Montreal.[19] This collaborative effort was facilitated by F. Cleveland Morgan, who played a central role in the Association during this period. Morgan was pivotal in expanding its collections of decorative art, and took charge of raising the money required to publish Traquair's study.

Interestingly, Traquair submitted his manuscript to Henry G. Birks, requesting comments, which Birks made in letters written in March and May of 1938.[20] Most had to do with the correction of factual errors, especially those pertaining to Henry Birks and Sons and its direct predecessors.

In addition to his research, Traquair assembled a modest collection of his own, acquiring his first pieces around 1930. He appears to have purchased most of them from the Montreal antique dealer H. Baron. The approximately forty items he

Fig. 6
Ramsay H. Traquair (1874–1952), in the refectory of the Hôpital-Général, Quebec City, around 1928.

gathered over the years were bequeathed to the Art Association in 1952, no doubt as an expression of gratitude for its role in the publication of his study. The Art Association has since become the Montreal Museum of Fine Arts, and these pieces are still part of its holdings.[21] They are mainly from Quebec but some are imported, of which the most significant is the *Ewer with Arms of the Le Gardeur de Repentigny and the Chaussegros de Léry Families* (fig. 7). Traquair's exemplary activities as a researcher and collector undoubtedly encouraged others to do the same. He seems to have had a direct impact on Henry G. Birks, inspiring him to undertake his great venture.

There is one last collection of silver that absolutely must be mentioned: that of Louis Carrier (1898–1962). On 17 December 1959, the Musée de la province de Québec acquired all 741 pieces of this collection by ministerial decree.[22] A native of Lévis, Carrier worked in the fields of publishing and advertising for most of his life and occupied the post of curator at the Château Ramezay in Montreal from 1954 to 1962.[23] Always passionately attracted to "early Quebec art," as it is called today, he very soon developed a specific interest in silver. Between 1920 and 1957, his professional activities required him to travel extensively throughout Quebec, and he took the opportunity to examine and acquire various items, always with the clear end in mind of gathering works by every early Quebec silversmith. Although he did not achieve this ambitious goal, he deserves much credit for his accomplishments. One of Carrier's significant contributions was his dedication to fundamental research. Hardly any publications dealt with Quebec silver at the time, which meant that the few collectors who existed were required to conduct their own research. Carrier is one who made every effort to ferret out documents to authenticate the pieces he considered acquiring. Another, unexamined aspect of Carrier's contribution is his role in the formation of the Henry Birks Collection – a subject we will return to later.

In the first half of the twentieth century interest in silver continued to grow, partly due to its inclusion in exhibitions, most of which explored broader themes and did not focus exclusively on silver. In 1905, the Montreal Branch of the Women's Art Association presented one of the most important of these shows, the *Exhibition of Canadian Handicrafts*, held in Montreal.[24] The exhibition encompassed various eras and a broad range of interests; the catalogue devotes 252 entries to early silver and other metals. Despite the limited information offered there, the exhibition is known to have included pieces from early Quebec, France, and England, lent by old Quebec families. The presentation enhanced the profile of silver collecting and may have fostered an increased interest in the field.

The annual exhibition of the Canadian Guild of Crafts in 1932 included an unusual stand installed by Ramsay Traquair and Cleveland Morgan with the assistance of Galt Durnford.[25] Very little is known about this display except that it presented Quebec silver, accompanied by sculpture and ironwork, all belonging to the three collectors. Several years later, in 1935, the Ontario Association of Architects presented a selection of Traquair's photographs of Quebec architecture and silver – the subjects of his two major publications – as part of the *Fifth Biennial Exhibition of Architecture and Allied Arts*.[26] These were mounted alongside some forty pieces of silver from private collections and religious institutions. Marius Barbeau, who helped organize the exhibition, took the opportunity to publish his article "Deux cents ans d'orfèvrerie chez nous" (two hundred years of silver in our country).[27] In 1940 the Canadian Guild of Crafts returned to this theme, holding another exhibition devoted to early silver with works contributed partly by members of the organization and partly by the McCord Museum.[28] A similar show was presented by the Art Association in 1941, *Arts of Old Quebec*, which displayed Quebec silver in the context of early sculpture, arrow sashes, paintings, and furniture.[29]

It is Gérard Morisset who deserves the credit for at last organizing a major "Ranvoyzé event" in 1942, which included an exhibition,[30] a published catalogue and monograph,[31] and a series of radio lectures.[32] For the first time the public could view an exhibition devoted exclusively to silver. The *Exposition de photographies d'argenteries québécoises: François Ranvoyzé (Québec, 1739 – Québec, 1819)*

Fig. 7
Jean Fauché
Paris 1706–1762
Ewer with Arms of the Le Gardeur de Repentigny and the Chaussegros de Léry Families 1754–55
Silver
Montreal Museum of Fine Arts, Bequest of Ramsay H. Traquair (1952.Ds.45)

(exhibition of photographs of Quebec silver: François Ranvoyzé [Quebec City, 1739–1819]) was first shown at the École des beaux-arts in Quebec City, then in Montreal, and finally at the Institut Français in New York. As the title suggests, most of the works (thirty-three) were by Ranvoyzé, but there were also five by Amiot. The monograph *François Ranvoyzé* should be regarded as the essential companion volume to the exhibition, which accounts for the cursory nature of the catalogue. Though quite modest, *François Ranvoyzé* is nonetheless the first published monograph on a Quebec silversmith.

To summarize, after having occupied a limited place in various exhibitions treating broader themes in the first third of the twentieth century, by the end of that same period early Quebec silver had emerged as a separate discipline, and publications on the topic began to see the light of day.

Henry Birks and Sons

Before examining Henry G. Birks's activities as a collector, let us briefly review the origins of the company, Henry Birks and Sons, whose activities played a determining role in his choice of acquisitions. The elder Henry Birks (1840–1928) was the son of John Birks and Anne Massey. A native of England, John had immigrated to Canada in 1832, establishing a business in Montreal, where Henry was born and raised. One year after completing his studies at Montreal High School in 1856, Henry was hired by the clockmakers and jewellers Savage and Lyman, whose store was considered the best of its kind in Canada. The economic crisis of 1873 dealt a severe blow to the company; it went bankrupt and was forced to close its doors in 1878.

The following year, on 1 March 1879, Henry Birks opened a small jewellery store of his own at 22 St James Street (now rue Saint-Jacques), in the heart of the business district. He immediately instituted new customer-service policies: cash only, and the same price for everyone. In 1885, Birks moved his store to a larger space at number 232 on the same street. A more fundamental change followed in 1893 when the founder brought his three sons – William Massey, John Henry, and Gerald – into the company, which then became Henry Birks and Sons. That same year they planned a move to Phillips Square, following the development of the city, and the newly constructed store opened its doors on the corner of St Catherine (Sainte-Catherine) and Union streets in 1894. In 1898, Henry Birks and Sons bought out Hendery and Leslie, which had been supplying Birks with silver since 1879. From this point on, the company was in a position to produce its own merchandise, which gave it more control over the market. At the same time, it made the decision to specialize in silver, which led to a growth in business and the expansion of its distribution network. Three years later, in 1901, after examining the volume of sales handled by its mail-order department, the company opened a store in Ottawa. This would prove to be the first of many outside of Montreal. By the start of the Second World War, through opening new stores and buying out existing ones across the country, Birks had come to monopolize the Canadian silver market. In this period the company purchased Olmsted and Hurman of Ottawa (1902), opened a store in Winnipeg (1903), and purchased Ryrie Brothers of Toronto (1905), George E. Trorey Limited of Vancouver (1906), Gorham Company Canada (1907), A. Rosenthal and Sons of Ottawa (1911), Porte and Markle of Winnipeg (1913), M.S. Brown and Company of Halifax (1919), and D.E. Black and Company of Calgary (1920). Continuing its expansion, Birks opened a store in London, England (1925), purchased D.A. Kirkland of Edmonton (1926), N.C. Maynard and Company of Hamilton (1927), W.G. Watson and Company of Saskatoon and Hamilton (1928), and J.E. Wilnot of Ottawa (1929), and opened a store in Antwerp, Belgium (1929). It then purchased G. Seifert and Sons of Quebec City (1930), Robertson and Company of Saint John, New Brunswick (1931), Ellis Brothers Limited of Toronto (1932), D.R. Dingwall Limited of Winnipeg (1933), and Percy R. Thomas of Edmonton (1935), and opened a store in Sudbury, Ontario (1938). The year 1943 saw the opening of a store in London, Ontario, and the purchase of Howard H. Patch of Montreal and W.H. McCreery of Windsor, Ontario.[33] In 1944, William Massey Birks's eldest son, Henry Gifford Birks, became president of the company. During his tenure, thirty new stores were opened across Canada.[34] Given that he presided over this pan-Canadian empire in an era that witnessed a growing interest in old silver, it is not surprising that the younger Birks gradually came to feel the need to explore the company's past, and, subsequently, the evolution of silver in Canada.

A slim volume published in 1925 appears to provide some early insights into the intentions behind the creation of the Henry Birks Collection, which began to take form a decade later. Written by J. Earl Birks, the vice-president of Ryrie-Birks Limited, *The Romance of Silver Craft* aimed to apply a patina of distinction to the Canadian company by tracing the art of silver-making from ancient times through the institution of the hallmark system in England to the cutlers named Birks who plied their trade in Sheffield, England, during the sixteenth, seventeenth, and eighteenth centuries. The last pages of this work make it very clear, with the aid of an illustration, that the tea service purchased today will become the precious family heirloom of tomorrow:

> One hundred years from now some happy bride-elect will take down from the family shelf, to grace the wedding breakfast, a treasured old tea service as unspoiled by time and fashion as on the day when her own great-grandmother unwrapped it and set it proudly at the head of all her wedding gifts in the year 1925.[35]

More than simply a promotional item, this publication attests to the company's desire to establish its place in history by attempting to trace the longest and most prestigious roots possible for the rapidly expanding empire. The bid to associate their firm with the revered English tradition was an eminently respectable undertaking in the Anglophile climate of 1925.

As mentioned above, Henry Birks read and commented on Ramsay Traquair's manuscript in the spring of 1938. The exercise led him to formulate a joint project, outlined in a series of letters exchanged over the next few months. Birks asked Traquair to extend the period examined in his original study, which focussed on the years 1750 through 1850, to the end of the nineteenth century, so as to cover the activities of Hendery and Leslie. In exchange, he was prepared to pay a portion of the publication costs and to make the book available in every store of the chain. In his reply Traquair emphasized that this publication, like all his previous ones, must present no grounds for doubt as to the independence of the researcher, and must at minimum meet with the approval of his university.[36] The book therefore needed to be published by an outside firm and distributed through normal channels. It appears Traquair did not want to be regarded as a spokesman for a commercial enterprise, a reservation Birks himself ultimately acknowledged as reasonable. In the upshot the book was published by the Art Association of Montreal, guaranteeing its moral authority. Birks's support for this initiative was part of the overall effort to enhance his company's prestige, in this case by presenting it as a continuation of the eighteenth- and nineteenth-century Quebec silversmithing tradition.

Published by Henry Birks and Sons in 1946, *The House of Birks* dispenses with equivocation. Probably as a result of his discussions with Traquair, Birks commissioned A. Robert George of the Department of Education at McGill University to write the book. The publisher's intentions are clearly stated in the introduction:

> It is the story of men and methods; dealing in precious metals and precious stones. This is an attempt to record origins, to mark the milestones on the way; and to introduce the men who founded the firm, and those who are carrying it on.[37]

Under the chapter heading "The Roots," the author has grouped a set of facts and assertions about the history of the company. For the first time, the introductory section traces a direct line from the Birks who were cutlers in England, to the arrival of John Birks in Canada, to the early years of Henry Birks, founder of the company. A second and third section continue the narrative. The second begins with Birks's hiring by Savage and Lyman and goes on to outline the history of this firm. The third and last section, entitled "Manufacturing the Silver," is broader in scope; it focusses on the most prominent Montreal silversmiths of the late eighteenth century and first half of the nineteenth, portraying them as the firm's precursors. The message of all three sections is bolstered by a generous selection of illustrations, including many portraits.

As one would expect, the "tree" nourished by these "roots" is the store on St James Street, which opened on 1 March 1879. The founding itself, however, is not described in great detail, and the lens rapidly shifts to focus on the company's development and expansion across Canada. The final section deals with the workshop, emphasizing the many years of service of its numerous employees. For example, photographs of eleven silversmiths are placed together on a single page and accompanied by the observation that they have contributed a total of 450 years of service to the firm. This short volume thus appears to be another attempt to appropriate the past, one that is bolder and somewhat more complex than the 1925 publication; by this time, Birks had already been building his silver collection for a decade.

The Collection

Henry G. Birks began his collecting project in 1936. It was entirely consistent with the initiatives described above. Initially, his goal was to bring together examples of the marks and the articles produced by the direct predecessors of the Birks workshop, that is, before 1898. The scope rapidly expanded, as will soon become evident. But why did he embark on his collection precisely in 1936? As already mentioned, there was a growing interest in silver, especially between 1930 and 1940. This interest was then heightened by an exhibition whose value and importance must not be underestimated: *British Silverwork by Well-Known Designers and Craftsmen of the Present Day Lent by the Worshipful Company of Goldsmiths of London.* This landmark show was held at Henry Birks and Sons in Montreal in March 1936, and then at Birks-Ellis-Ryrie in Toronto during the first two weeks of April; it presented approximately one hundred pieces, both solid silver and silver-plated, as well as some in glass and chrome.[38] Organized by Henry G. Birks himself in conjunction with Goldsmiths' Hall in London, this event apparently acted as a catalyst, for shortly thereafter he began to act on his ideas. In May 1936, he purchased his first piece, a *Kidney Brochette* (NGC 24014) by Quebec silversmith James Godfrey Hanna (c. 1737–1807), which, like his next acquisitions, was bought in London.

The accession book kept by the collector throughout this period is remarkable in many respects.[39] It provides a wealth of detail, but most importantly, outlines the way in which Birks conceived his project. The book is divided into eleven distinct categories, based on the provenance of each item or, in exceptional cases, the manufacturer. They are, in order: Quebec, Canada, Savage, Unknown, American, Maritimes, Hendery and Leslie, Birks, English, Foreign, and Australia. Quebec silver, which constitutes the most important part of the collection in terms of quantity, is further separated into five more sections depending on source: Quebec City, Montreal, the Hendery and Leslie workshop, the Savage firm, and Henry Birks and Sons. All pieces from the Maritimes are listed together, notwithstanding the province of origin, while those from Ontario are included in the section devoted to Canadian silver, which contains pieces from Montreal for the most part.

American, English, foreign, and Australian pieces, mainly small objects and flat-ware, are gathered into subgroups that appear to have been created responsively rather than as a specific intention. Some of the items had been considered Canadian until research proved otherwise, others were acquired for the purposes of study or comparison, and still others were received as gifts on various occasions.

Birks defined the principal categories from the start, that is, between May 1936 and May 1938, indicating that his focus was clear from the outset and not the result of either chance or a subsequent reorientation. If he had set out to concentrate on the direct precursors of his firm, a continuing goal, he soon had evidence that they were indeed part of a long and rich tradition. His range of interests quickly expanded to include Quebec silver from all eras, and he embarked on a passionate search for collectible items.

As each piece or set was acquired, he made an entry in the accession book, giving the work a name and number, and indicating the provenance, acquisition date, and cost, as relevant. At first he only recorded the weight, but later entered the dimensions as well. Engraved motifs were noted or described, as were the marks on early acquisitions. The names of the silversmiths and manufacturers were also recorded, and, when pieces and marks were photographed, the numbers of the negatives.

Birks purchased silver from many different sources, mainly in Canada but overseas as well, and mostly between May 1936 and September 1979. Some of his suppliers played a decisive role in the development and orientation of the collection. One such person, John E. Langdon (1902–1981), is well known for his writings on the marks of Canadian silversmiths.[40] Although he himself owned a collection of over five hundred pieces, mainly flatware (now at the Royal Ontario Museum), Langdon was also a dealer. In this capacity, he was among the first to have business contacts with Birks, starting in 1938, when Langdon was living in Montreal, and continuing after the latter's move to Toronto in 1950. Most of their transactions took place between 1938 and 1952, resulting in the addition of ninety-nine works to the collection. Over exactly the same period, Birks also established ties with Leslie R. Thomson, purchasing eighty-two items. In addition, Jean Palardy sold him twenty-two pieces between 1938 and 1942.[41]

In the early years, Birks concentrated on the acquisition of flatware, choosing items partly on the basis of their marks. Not until 1940, when Traquair published his study, was any guide to Canadian marks available, so at some undetermined time Birks drew up his own list for personal use in seeking out pieces.[42] The decade 1940 to 1950 saw the entry on the scene of new contacts, thanks to whom the collection became what it is today. In particular, the year 1940 marked the beginning of his transactions with the antique dealer H. Baron, from Montreal; these continued until 1972. Over that time, Birks acquired a total of 239 pieces. This significant portion of the collection includes not only flatware, but many liturgical objects as well. Among the remarkable pieces acquired from Baron are

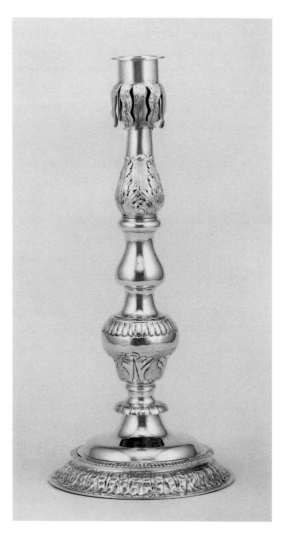

Fig. 8
Paul Lambert, *dit* Saint-Paul
Arras, France 1691? – Quebec City 1749
Altar Candlestick c. 1729–49
Silver
NGC, Gift of the Henry Birks Collection of
Canadian Silver, 1979 (24001)

the *Ecuelle Cover* (NGC 24127.2) by François Ranvoyzé (1739–1819) and the *Tea Service* (NGC 24133.1–4) by Robert Cruickshank (c. 1748–1809) and Peter Arnoldi (1769–before 1808), purchased in 1950 and 1970 respectively.

It was also during this period, in 1941, that Birks established business ties with Louis Carrier, which were to continue for two decades until 1961. Perhaps to finance his own collection, Carrier sold Birks 399 pieces. Most of the transactions took place in 1941, 1952, and 1954. Through this prestigious middleman, he added some key works to the collection, including the *Altar Candlestick* (fig. 8) by Paul Lambert (1691 or 1703–1749), acquired in 1949. The matching French candlestick remained in the Carrier collection and entered the Musée du Québec along with the rest in 1959.[43]

In 1948, Birks began to deal with Donald C. Mackay of Halifax. By 1977, he had bought forty-three items, mainly flatware by Maritime silversmiths. Mackay

Fig. 9
Jacques Pagé, *dit* Quercy
Quebec City 1682–1742
Ciborium c. 1720–25
Silver and gold
NGC, Gift of the Henry Birks Collection of Canadian Silver, 1979 (24347)

was his only important supplier in the Atlantic provinces. Like Carrier, Mackay was a collector in his own right. He also conducted research on the silversmiths of New Brunswick, Nova Scotia, Prince Edward Island, and Newfoundland. His publication on the subject appeared in 1973.[44]

In the late 1950s, another key player came on the scene, Montreal antique dealer Samuel Breitman. From 1957 to 1977, Birks purchased 450 articles from Breitman, which is more than he acquired from any other source. This portion of the collection includes flatware, numerous liturgical objects, and several pieces of tableware. Among the many fine pieces that entered the collection by this route are the famous *Ciborium* (fig. 9) by Jacques Pagé, *dit* Quercy (1682–1742), acquired in 1967, and the exceptional Neo-Classical *Chalice* (fig. 10) by François Sasseville (1797–1864), purchased in late 1969.

In the 1960s, Birks made contact with several new merchants. He purchased a total of 207 pieces from Herbert T. Schwartz, Jean Octeau, Rosaire St-Pierre, and Charles Poudrier, but perhaps the most important items were those bought from the Montrealers Harry M. Allice and John L. Russell. Between 1965 and 1979, Allice sold Birks 200 more pieces, notably a selection of items purchased in 1971 that included punches used by François Sasseville and Pierre Lespérance (1819–1882) for stamping their marks, another die employed by Lespérance to make soup spoons, and brass moulds for casting historiated motifs to ornament sacred vessels (fig. 11). Originally acquired from the J. Arsène Belleville company in Quebec City by Baron, these objects had been purchased by Carrier, who sold them to Allice, who sold them to Birks. Between 1967 and 1976, Birks purchased 165 pieces from the other Montreal dealer, John L. Russell. Thanks to his contacts with the descendants of several old families, Russell had been able to procure some important pieces of domestic silver, which he sold to Birks, including such key items as the *Plate with the Monogram of the Duperron Bâby Family* (fig. 12) by Paul Lambert, which came from the Monk estate, the *Tea Set with Arms of the Coffin Family* (NGC 24011.1–4) by Salomon Marion, supplied by a descendant of the original owner, and the *Sauce-boat* (fig. 13) by Pierre Huguet, *dit* Latour (1749–1817), acquired from descendants of the Bâby family then living in California.

On occasion, Henry Birks himself dealt directly with long-established Quebec families who, for one reason or another, had decided to part with silver heirlooms acquired or commissioned by their ancestors. In 1969, such dealings led to the acquisition of silver flatware bearing the monogram of the Saint-Ours family (NGC 24530–31; 25851–56), including a beaker inscribed with the name Virginie de Saint-Ours (NGC 24078), most of the items made by Peter Bohle (1786–1862) for George Savage and Son of Montreal in the mid-nineteenth century. These joined certain other pieces purchased as early as 1939 and also engraved with the Saint-Ours family monogram: a *Ladle* (NGC 24292) by Cruickshank and a *Serving Spoon* (NGC 25124) by Frederick Delisle (1796–after 1831). Five years later, in 1974, the collector succeeded in acquiring an exceptional piece: the *Ewer of*

Fig. 10
François Sasseville
Sainte-Anne-de-la-Pocatière, Quebec 1797 – Quebec City 1864
Chalice c. 1850
Silver and gold
NGC, Gift of the Henry Birks Collection of Canadian Silver, 1979 (24616)

Fig. 11

Silver Moulds

NGC, Gift of the Henry Birks Collection of Canadian Silver, 1979 (27742.4, 27742.6, 27741.1, 27741.5)

These four brass moulds, from a group of eleven undoubtedly acquired in Europe, are among those used by Quebec City silversmiths in the second half of the nineteenth century to make the historiated medallions that ornamented the calyces of chalices and ciboria (oval moulds) as well as the bases of chalices (triangular mould). They represent, above, *The Crucifixion,* and below, from left to right, *Mary Magdalen, Saint Joseph,* and *The Renunciation of Saint Peter.*

Fig. 12
Paul Lambert, *dit* Saint-Paul
Arras, France 1691? – Quebec City 1749
Plate with the Monogram of the Duperron Bâby Family c. 1729–49
Silver
NGC, Gift of the Henry Birks Collection of Canadian Silver, 1979 (25306)

François Ranvoyzé (fig. 14), which had remained in the artist's family until its last owner, before Birks, had received it as a wedding gift in 1942.[45]

Although the primary locus of the collector's activities was Canada itself, and particularly Montreal, he also repatriated a number of works that had left the country. As noted above, he bought his very first pieces from London dealers in the spring of 1936. Birks maintained and developed his business relationships with London merchants who specialized in early silver, and purchased many important works from them over a forty-year period. In the early years, the articles were offered to the manager of Henry Birks and Sons in London, who would then forward the offers to Montreal. As early as 1936, the *Beaker of Captain John Neill*

Fig. 13
Pierre Huguet, *dit* Latour
Quebec City 1749 – Montreal 1817
Sauce-boat c. 1788–1817
Silver
NGC, Gift of the Henry Birks Collection of Canadian Silver, 1979 (24098)

(NGC 24118) by Nelson Walker (1799–after 1855) was acquired in this way. The following year, a similar arrangement led to the acquisition of the *Montreal Agricultural Society Cup* (fig. 15) by Salomon Marion.

But perhaps the most significant piece brought back from Great Britain was the *Mortar* (fig. 16) by Paul Lambert which entered the collection in January 1948 – the only such mortar known to have been made in Quebec. It was created for the Jesuit college in Quebec City, undoubtedly for the pharmacist, sometime between 1729 and 1749. After the death of Jean-Joseph Casot in 1800, the mortar was transferred to the Monastère des Hospitalières de l'Hôtel-Dieu de Québec.[46] In 1881, the nuns at the Hôtel-Dieu sent it to Lespérance, requesting that it be melted down and forged into pectoral reliquary crosses. Before this could happen, the Marquess of Lorne, Governor General of Canada at the time, acquired the mortar from the silversmith that same year, with the intention of giving it to his wife, Princess Louise, as a souvenir of the Hôtel-Dieu de Québec.[47] In 1947, Marius Barbeau of the Canadian Museum of Civilization, then the National Museum of

Fig. 14
François Ranvoyzé
Quebec City 1739–1819
Ewer of François Ranvoyzé c. 1770–80
Silver
NGC, Gift of the Henry Birks Collection of Canadian Silver, 1979 (27775)

Fig. 15
Salomon Marion
Lachenaie, Quebec 1782 – Montreal 1830
Montreal Agricultural Society Cup c. 1820
Silver and gold
NGC, Gift of the Henry Birks Collection of
Canadian Silver, 1979 (24139)

Man, and F. St George Spendlove of the Royal Ontario Museum both learned that a London dealer was in possession of the mortar.[48] Spendlove had passed this information on to Birks, who then acquired the piece and immediately deposited it at the ROM. The *Mortar* remained on display in Toronto throughout the next four decades (1948–88), before being sent to the National Gallery of Canada for the inauguration of its new building. In addition to maintaining his British contacts, Birks developed business relationships in the United States, which also led to certain discoveries and important acquisitions. For example, in January 1947 he purchased the *Ewer* (fig. 17) by David Bohle (1831–1869) from a New York art dealer. Other such opportunities arose at later dates.

As we have seen, Henry Birks had ongoing contact with a great many dealers and collectors here and abroad in the decades during which he was assembling his collection. Characteristically, on various occasions other Quebec silver collections

Fig. 16
Paul Lambert, *dit* Saint-Paul
Arras, France 1691? – Quebec City 1749
Mortar c. 1729–49
Silver
NGC, Gift of the Henry Birks Collection of Canadian Silver, 1979 (24501)

or significant portions of them were incorporated into his. The first such occurrence was in 1947, when he acquired eleven pieces from the estate of Francis Patrick Garvan (1875–1937). Born in East Hartford, Connecticut, Garvan was the son of a Hartford paper manufacturer. In the middle of the first decade of this century, he started collecting Colonial decorative art. The collection grew phenomenally, reaching a total of ten thousand objects. It contained silver, furniture, pewter, ceramics, glass, brassware, ironware, textiles, coins, engravings, and paintings, including many important works. They are now at the Yale University Art Gallery, where they form the Mabel Brady Garvan Collection, named after the collector's wife.[49]

Garvan put a great deal of money and energy into organizing a remarkable set of American silver, which became one of the jewels in the overall collection. He also acquired a set of pieces described as "Catholic Silver from Canada" from E. Alfred Jones.[50] The two men had exchanged letters since at least 1926,[51] when Jones was preparing a volume to be published in 1928, *Old Silver of Europe and America*. They closed the deal in the autumn of 1929, which Jones spent in the United States. Garvan's interest in Roman Catholic liturgical silver probably stemmed from his own Irish Catholic background. He may also have hoped that adding some Quebec silver to his vast American collection would put it in some kind of perspective. The small group contained eleven pieces, including the exceptional *Ewer Belonging to Abbé Louis-Michel Bériau* (NGC 27774) by François Ranvoyzé.[52] In all probability, Jones purchased these works when visiting Quebec City in 1912, at which time he apparently acquired other pieces as well, whose whereabouts are currently unknown.[53]

Shortly after acquiring it, Garvan deposited the "Catholic Silver" at the Yale University Art Gallery in New Haven. In 1947, while the details of his estate were finally being settled, the gallery decided not to retain them, and consequently got in touch with the Royal Ontario Museum in Toronto. Intense negotiations then ensued between Spendlove and Birks, Spendlove aiming to persuade the latter to purchase the silver and donate it to the museum. At last he agreed to do this, and deposited it at the ROM in 1947. Although the National Gallery of Canada became its legal owner in 1979, having been given the Henry Birks Collection that year, certain works from the initial deposit are still on exhibit in Toronto.

An interesting sidelight to this story is that, in January 1948, when a sanctuary lamp by Amiot (NGC 27574) was sent from New Haven to Toronto, it was accompanied by an exceptional, in fact unique, group of drawings: twenty-two sheets comprising twenty-eight designs for religious silver, most of them by Amiot (see fig. 18). They were in all likelihood acquired by Jones in 1912 while visiting the son of Ambroise Lafrance (1847–1905).[54]

The Garvan collection also included three ciboria, two from France and one from Liège, purchased by Birks subject to special terms, which meant they did not become the property of the National Gallery in 1979 but were instead on deposit

Fig. 17
David Bohle
Montreal 1831–1869
Ewer c. 1850–60
Silver
NGC, Gift of the Henry Birks Collection of Canadian Silver, 1979 (24093)

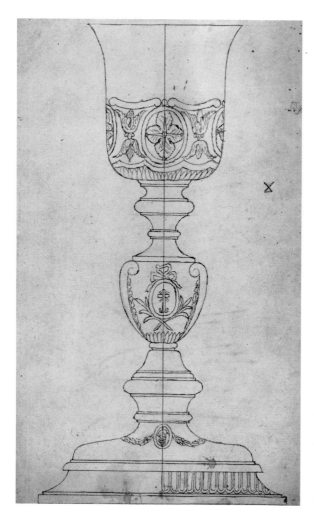

Fig. 18
Laurent Amiot
Quebec City 1764–1839
Design for a Chalice c. 1825
Black ink on laid paper
Royal Ontario Museum, Toronto
(948.279.16)

at the Royal Ontario Museum until 1985, and since then at the Musée du Séminaire de Québec in Quebec City (now the Musée de l'Amérique française).[55] The ROM is also the final home of a set of twenty-three silver pieces from England, which he bought in 1960 and immediately deposited at the museum, donating them as a gift in 1983.

In June 1965, an auction took place in Toronto to sell off most of the various collections assembled by Joseph H. Bauer of Waterloo, Ontario.[56] As well as furniture, porcelain, books, paintings, and other items, there were a number of lots of silver items. Naturally, Birks focussed his efforts on acquiring the Quebec silver, though he also acquired a *Ciborium* (NGC 27850) by Peter Nordbeck (1789–1861) of Saint John, New Brunswick. With Breitman as middleman, he purchased ten lots, thus acquiring the unique *Butter Dish* (NGC 24931) by Lespérance, and, most notably, the outstanding *Ewer* (fig. 4) by Amiot, which soon became one of the visual reference points of his collection.

The same basic scenario was repeated, again in Toronto, in the spring of 1979, when the Charles De Volpi Canadian silver collection went on the auction block.[57] The 237 lots on offer contained mostly flatware. Eight pieces, including the last items of Quebec silver to enter the collection, were purchased, one of them a jewel of the De Volpi collection, the remarkable *Spice Box* by Laurent Amiot (NGC 27079), which appears to be one of a kind in Canada.

Cyrille Tessier, mentioned at the beginning of the chapter, was one of Quebec's first silver collectors – using the term rather broadly, since some of the flatware in his collection bore the monogram of his father, Michel Tessier. Other pieces, without an inscription, could have been purchased by either man, judging by their production dates. Whether they were family possessions or subsequent acquisitions by Cyrille (it is difficult at present to establish the precise origin of each item), the pieces forming the Tessier collection were divided among family members, probably after his death in 1931. In 1971, his granddaughter sold her share to Henry Birks: forty-two items, divided into eighteen distinct groups, of which the most remarkable were the *Sauce Tureen* by Amiot (see fig. 5) and the *Pair of Sauce-boats* (NGC 27852.1–2) by Lespérance. Birks had already bought the large *Ewer* by Amiot in 1965 (see fig. 4), several years before purchasing this elegant set. Although he bought the ewer at the Bauer collection sale, it had previously belonged to Carrier, who had himself acquired it from Joachim des Rivières Tessier, son of Cyrille Tessier.

Overall, then, the Henry Birks Collection is a synthesis of silver articles from a multitude of sources, which increased in number and diversity, the collection growing more specialized as the collector's intentions became more clearly defined and better known among his peers.

The Deposit Program

The owner of this enormous collection (7091 objects in 3970 groupings) soon became preoccupied with making it better known. One of the ways he went about this was to deposit selected works at Canadian museums that already possessed Quebec silver and desired to supplement their collections, or at museums that did not own any silver but expressed an interest in the field. These deposits made it possible for the public to view most of the Birks Collection's key works on a con-tinuous basis. In fact, because of their unique character or superior quality, many significant pieces were distributed in this manner as soon as they were purchased. The deposits were always flexible, the institution keeping the possibility of mod-ifying them according to their desires, and especially according to the evolution of the collection the deposit was intended to complete, as well as to changes in its overall exhibition policies.

Predictably, the first deposit was placed at the Art Association of Montreal, now the Montreal Museum of Fine Arts, as early as February 1940.[58] The friendship between F. Cleveland Morgan and Henry G. Birks, nourished by their shared and sustained interest in the vernacular, undoubtedly paved the way. At the time, the Art Association's collection was small, but Birks hoped by his loan to encourage further institutional initiatives. Individual pieces were added over the years, and the entire deposit was reorganized in 1947, when the large *Ewer* by David Bohle was deposited (see fig. 17), and again in 1955, 1962, and 1992. This last change was implemented to round out the museum's collection, which has grown spectacularly since the first deposit was made nearly sixty years ago.

The deposit at the Royal Ontario Museum dates back to 1948, in the context of the purchase by Birks of Quebec silver from the Garvan Collection – inspired by Spendlove, who was greatly attached to the Garvan collection and would have very much liked to acquire it for the museum. Paying homage to Spendlove's passion and determination, Birks left these works on deposit at the ROM for many years. Most of them, in fact, are still there. Other pieces have been added to the deposit over the years, lending diversity to the presentation of silver at the museum at the same time that it has been developing its own collection, notably with the help of gifts from the collector John E. Langdon.

The following year, 1949, Birks deposited several pieces at the Archives de la province de Québec in Quebec City, through an agreement with the archivist, Antoine Roy.[59] At this time, the archives were located in the same building as the Musée de la province de Québec in the Parc des Champs-de-Bataille; the institutions had separate displays of their permanent collections. Substantial additions were made to this deposit in 1951 and 1964. In 1967, one year after Jean Trudel was named curator of traditional art at the Musée du Québec, he asked for and was granted the transfer of the deposit from the archives to the Musée. The works were finally returned to Henry Birks and Sons in 1974, the richness of the Musée's own collection at that point undoubtedly serving as justification for discontinuing the loan.

In the mid-1950s, Birks placed three new deposits, at the Art Gallery of Hamilton in 1955,[60] the Château Ramezay in Montreal in 1955,[61] and the New Brunswick Museum in Saint John in 1956.[62] The Art Gallery of Hamilton's interest in early Quebec silver may have had something to do with the presentation of large exhibitions of early Quebec art in the neighbouring city of Detroit in 1946 and 1951. Whatever the cause, the gallery presented *A Selection from the Louis Carrier Collection of Canadian Silver*, from its own collection, in 1953. The deposit of items from the Birks collection two years later was a logical encouragement of the gallery's undeniable interest in the field. Due to changes in policy, the deposit was returned in 1993, and the pieces have not been shown for several years.

Coincidentally, the same Louis Carrier, who had just been named curator of the Château Ramezay, obtained a deposit of twenty-two religious pieces from the Birks Collection in June 1955 for his institution. The deposit was modified in 1967 and again in 1971, and the museum finally returned it, now comprising twenty-four items, in 1981.

The 1956 deposit at the New Brunswick Museum, a response to a request by George MacBeath of the Department of Canadian History, contained seven pieces. Except for one work by William Herman Newman (1826–1894) of Saint John, all were from Quebec. Perhaps the institution wished to thus broaden the context of appreciation for its own silver collection. After some changes in 1964, the deposit was returned to Montreal around 1973.

As part of his continuing loan policy, Birks sent thirty-two works to Saskatoon to be exhibited at the Mendel Art Gallery in December 1964.[63] The pieces remained there until the summer of 1982, when they were returned to the Gallery.

In November 1975, Birks lent twenty-six pieces to the Musée d'art de Joliette for an exhibition that was to continue until May 1976.[64] After several renewals, the loan was converted into a deposit. In 1981, by which time the National Gallery owned the collection, substitutions began of several works, and two years later the museum returned the remaining pieces to Ottawa.

In 1976, the David M. Stewart Museum, then the Montreal Military and Maritime Museum, received four pieces of fur-trade silver intended to complete its collection.[65] They are still there today.

The following year, 1977, Queen Elizabeth II visited Ottawa for the festivities around the twenty-fifth anniversary of her accession to the throne. To mark the event, the Birks deposited sixty-eight works at Rideau Hall, the residence of the Governor General, which were to be displayed in areas accessible to the public.[66] The selection consisted mostly of pieces from Quebec, covering practically every period, but also included several works from the Maritimes and one from Toronto dating from the late nineteenth century. Despite modifications, the core of the original selection remained unchanged until the summer of 1990, when the works came back to the National Gallery, following a renovation of Rideau Hall's public areas.

The same year, 1977, seven pieces were lent to the Canadian Museum of Civilization for an initial period of five years.[67] As usual, the deposit was adapted to the museum's changing needs, to such an extent that only one work from the original deposit remains there today, while eleven new ones have been added.

Finally, in 1984, the National Gallery of Canada, in the same spirit that guided the collector, agreed to deposit a number of pieces at the Musée d'art de Saint-Laurent for an exhibition on silversmithing techniques.[68] This furnished the occasion to make some of the tools of the trade accessible to the public, comprising seven burnishers, a file, and eleven moulds used by Quebec smiths in the nineteenth century. Here again, changes in the Musée's permanent display led to the return of the pieces to Ottawa in the winter of 1997.

The deposit formula, one of Birks's favourite methods of highlighting his collection, was used mainly from 1940 to 1970. It proved an invaluable aid to those museums that strove to foster an appreciation of silverwork but did not have sufficiently large collections to do so. However, a recent trend among museums towards placing more emphasis on temporary exhibitions than on permanent displays led many smaller institutions to lose interest in the deposit mechanism, although larger ones continued to use it to readjust their already substantial collections.

The Exhibitions

In addition to this active and sustained deposit policy, Birks generously lent pieces to numerous exhibitions, from the time he began collecting until the time of the donation to the National Gallery. While it would be tedious to list them all, we should mention that, at the moment when the deposit formula began to wane in the seventies, a number of exhibitions were organized specifically around the Henry Birks Collection. The selection presented in 1970 at La Maison Del Vecchio in Old Montreal, *The Silver Thread through Canadian History: The Henry Birks Collection of Canadian Silver*,[69] foreshadowed the exhibition presented the following year in St John's, Newfoundland, at the Arts and Culture Centre.[70] In fact, like the preceding one, *The Newfoundland Historic Trust Antiques Exhibition* displayed some 150 works, mainly by Quebec silversmiths. As a complement, about 100 items of flatware were also exhibited, positioned to expose the marks of the smiths working in the main centres of the Maritimes and Ontario, as well as in Quebec City and Montreal. The Newfoundland exhibition also included a selection of engravings and local furniture.

Several years later, in 1974, the Winnipeg Art Gallery presented *The Development of Canadian Silver*.[71] This exhibition differed in one way from the two before it: though it presented an impressive total of 193 works, some borrowed from other collections, and though the emphasis was still on Quebec silver, not as many maker's marks were on display as in the previous two shows.

In 1976, The Heraldry Society of Canada held the small but highly significant *Exhibition of Armorial Silver from the Henry Birks Collection of Canadian Silver* at the National Archives of Canada.[72] The organizers took the presentation of silverwork in a new direction, abandoning the broad survey, which had dominated previous exhibitions, to isolate one well-defined area of research. Here, they studied and described the arms featured on thirty-one works. *A Sterling Past: The Silversmiths of Canada*, presented in Victoria at the Royal British Columbia Provincial Museum in 1978, and then in Calgary, Edmonton, and Vancouver,[73] was similar to those of 1970 and 1974 in the number of works displayed (158 in this case), but the pieces appear to have been grouped together more systematically, according to seven categories mapped out by specialists of the period and based on stylistic influences, types of work, and geographic origin. Twenty-three tools were also displayed – apparently the first time silversmithing equipment was included within an exhibition of silver pieces.

The same year also witnessed the presentation of *Historic Canadian Silver from The Henry Birks Collection* in Toronto, first at the Art Gallery of York University, and then at Henry Birks and Sons in the Toronto Eaton Centre.[74] The eighty-three pieces in this wide-ranging exhibition were made by many different Quebec silversmiths, though emphasis was placed on key figures. The works apparently were chosen for their intrinsic qualities. This was the last show devoted to the Henry Birks Collection before it was given to the National Gallery of Canada.

The gift inspired the National Gallery to mount a travelling exhibition with an accompanying catalogue, *Presentation Pieces and Trophies from the Henry Birks Collection of Canadian Silver*, in 1985.[75] Certainly, the Gallery wished to show its appreciation to the donors of this prestigious collection. However, rather than simply present a broad survey, the curator, Ross Allan C. Fox, chose to focus on a selected group of important and characteristic works. His decision signals a turn, already foreshadowed by the initiative of The Heraldry Society of Canada, away from the overview and towards the study of one particular branch of early silver – in this case, a branch neglected up until then. By the same gesture, the entire silver production of the second half of the nineteenth century was brought back into the light of scholarship. It was thus an excellent introduction to the Henry Birks collection, the Canadian collection with the greatest number of honorific and presentation pieces.

One of the ways in which Birks encouraged the development of knowledge of silver was by making his collection accessible to scholars. We have already mentioned that, as early as 1938, he offered comments on Traquair's manuscript. In 1960, he collaborated closely with Langdon on the publication of *Canadian Silversmiths and Their Marks, 1667–1867*, contributing lists of silversmith's marks and most of the photographs illustrating the volume. He displayed the same interest and generosity during the preparation of Langdon's *Canadian Silversmiths, 1700–1900*, published in 1966, and bought twenty-five copies after considering taking a hundred.[76]

During its history, the Birks Collection has been widely shared, first in the form of deposits at a variety of Canadian museums, and then through many exhibitions, whether drawn from the collection alone or in the context of shows covering broader themes. In 1979, Henry Birks and Sons celebrated the one-hundredth anniversary of its founding. In the spirit of Henry Gifford Birks himself, the firm wished to thank the people of Canada for a century of support. Consequently, on 14 December of the same year, the company donated the entire Henry Birks Collection of Canadian Silver to the National Gallery of Canada, which, by a happy coincidence, was just about to celebrate its own centennial in 1980.

Notes

1. Elwood 1983–84.

2. Allodi 1974, pp. 7–9.

3. Cooke 1983, pp. xiii–xv.

4. Ibid., pp. xv–xvi. The Public Archives of Canada officially became the National Archives of Canada on 11 June 1987.

5. *William Hugh Coverdale* 1980, p. 28.

6. Conversation in the summer of 1983 between the author and Philippe Treffry, librarian at the Musée du Québec, Quebec City, at the time.

7. *William Hugh Coverdale* 1980, p. 57.

8. Gauvreau 1940a, pp. 527–32.

9. IBC, Gérard Morisset fonds: Montreal, École du Meuble (Coll: Paul Gouin); list drawn up 22 September 1943.

10. *Musée du Québec* 1983, p. 49.

11. Chassay 1988.

12. ANQQ, register of notary Antoine-Archange Parent, no. 8930, 14 December 1841, testament of Monseigneur Joseph Signaÿ.

13. The customary pastoral visit normally required the bishop to inspect the condition of the churches' sacred vessels. The account books of the many parishes of the Quebec diocese, over which Joseph Signaÿ presided, reveal the painstaking care with which he carried out this portion of his duties. He never hesitated to insist on having a chalice regilded or commissioning a second ciborium. In Charlesbourg in 1837, he even had a pyx and baptismal jug recast (see Archives, council of churchwardens, Saint-Charles-Borromée, Charlesbourg, accounts and minutes, vol. 3 [1775–1841], 1837, n.p.)

14. Roy 1933, pp. 138–40.

15. See Villeneuve 1983, pp. 320, 325–27, 335, and 377.

16. Jones 1913.

17. Archives, Canadian Guild of Crafts. "Chronology for Ramsay Traquair: Biographical Details and Related Events" (C6D10131926).

18. See Derome 1987b.

19. Traquair 1940.

20. NGC curatorial archives, notes by Henry G. Birks, 8 and 9 February, 9 and 24 March, and 1 November 1938; letter from Henry G. Birks to Ramsay Traquair, 20 May 1938.

21. Ramsay Traquair bequeathed the following pieces to the Montreal Museum of Fine Arts:
    Peter Arnoldi, *Snuffbox* (1952.Ds.20)
    Paul Lambert, *dit* Saint Paul, and Samuel Payne, *Ecuelle* (1952.Ds.20)
    Robert Hendery, *Holy Water Pail* (1952.Ds.21a)
    Robert Hendery, *Sprinkler* (1952.Ds.21b)
    Charles-François Delique, *Beaker* (1952.Ds24)
    Joseph Mailloux, *Cup* (1952.Ds.25)
    Ignace-François Delezenne, *Cup* (1952.Ds.26)
    Anonymous (Canadian), *Cup* (1952.Ds.27)
    Anonymous (Canadian), *Cup* (1952.Ds.28)
    Guillaume Baudry, *dit* Des Buttes, *Wine Taster* (1952.Ds.29)
    Guillaume Baudry, *dit* Des Buttes, *Spoon* (1952.Ds.30)
    François Ranvoyzé, *Tray for Cruets* (1952.Ds31)
    François Ranvoyzé, *Spoon* (1952.Ds.32)

François Ranvoyzé, *Incense-boat* (1952.Ds.33)
Pierre Huguet, *dit* Latour, *Ciborium* (1952.Ds.34a-b)
Pierre Huguet, *dit* Latour, *Ciborium* (1952.Ds.35a-b)
Pierre Huguet, *dit* Latour, *Holy Water Pail* (1952.Ds.36)
Pierre Huguet, *dit* Latour, *Incense-boat* (1952.Ds.37)
Pierre Huguet, *dit* Latour, *Milk Jug* (1952.Ds.38)
Pierre Huguet, *dit* Latour, *Chrismatory* (1952.Ds.39)
Robert Cruickshank, *Chalice* (1952.Ds.40)
Laurent Amiot, *Teapot* (1952.Ds.41)
Henry Polonceau, *Baptismal Jug and Stand* (1952.Ds.42a-b)
Anonymous, *Sugar Tongs* (1952.Ds.43)
François Sasseville, *Baptismal Jug* (1952.Ds.44)
Jean Fauché, *Ewer with Arms of the Le Gardeur de Repentigny and the Chaussegros de Léry Families* (1952.Ds.45)
Anonymous, *Chalice* (1952.Ds.46)
Charles-François Delique, *Ampoula for Holy Oil* (1952.Ds.47)
Anonymous, *Bowl* (1952.Ds.48)
Anonymous, *Spoon* (1952.Ds.49)
James Eastwood, *Mustard Ladle* (1952.Ds.51)
Nathaniel Starnes, *Ladle* (1952.Ds.52)
Ambroise Lafrance, *Dessert Spoon* (1952.Ds.53)
Gervais Laffite, *Spoon* (1952.Ds.58)
Anonymous (France), *Spoon* (1952.Ds.59)
Anonymous (France), *Fork* (1952.Ds.60)

22. Villeneuve 1983, pp. 308–09.

23. Corbeil 1954.

24. *Exhibition of Canadian Handicrafts* 1905. Held under the auspices of the Montreal Branch of the Women's Art Association (chartered in 1906 as the Canadian Handicrafts Guild, and now the Canadian Guild of Crafts, Quebec).

25. "Exhibition, 1932" 1933.

26. *Fifth Biennial Exhibition* 1935.

27. Barbeau 1939c.

28. *Canadian Handicrafts Guild* 1941.

29. "Arts of Old Quebec" 1941.

30. Morisset 1942a.

31. Morisset 1942b.

32. Morisset gave a series of eight lectures, entitled *L'orfèvrerie au Canada français* (silver of French Canada) during the first season of *Radio-Collège* (radio college), broadcast on Radio-Canada, 1941–42. See *Radio-Collège* 1941, pp. 16–18.

33. George 1946.

34. MacLeod 1979, pp. 37–49.

35. Birks 1925.

36. NGC curatorial archives, note from Henry G. Birks, 24 March 1938.

37. George 1946, p. 1.

38. See Library of Goldsmiths' Hall, file 9/1178, "Exhibitions Abroad 1936 Canada (Henry Birks and Sons)." The author would like to thank Peter Kaellgren, Curator, Department of Western Art and Culture, Royal Ontario Museum, for providing this information.

39. NGC curatorial archives, accession book of the Henry Birks Collection of Canadian Silver, n.p. (photocopy).

40. See De Pencier 1982.

41. Jean Palardy himself acquired a small collection of silver. In 1983 he gave twenty-four pieces to the Musée d'art de Saint-Laurent. See *Hommage à Jean Palardy* 1984, catalogue numbers 2–25.

42. NGC curatorial archives, handwritten list of Canadian silversmiths' marks (six binders), n.d.

43. The *Altar Candlestick* at the Musée du Québec (A.60.263.0) was made by an unknown Parisian silversmith in 1674–75. On 17 December 1959, the Musée, then the Musée de la province de Québec, Quebec City, acquired the Carrier collection by ministerial decree.

44. See Mackay 1973.

45. The provenance of this vase is rather special, since it was not only produced by Ranvoyzé but belonged to him as well as his descendants; his initials, *FR*, are inscribed on the large cartouche engraved on the belly. Genealogical study reveals that the *Ewer*, which belonged to François Ranvoyzé and his wife, Vénérande Pellerin, was passed down to their daughter, Vénérande, who married Joseph DeBlois, a wealthy Quebec City merchant. The piece was then inherited by their daughter, Vénérande-Joséphine, who married René-Édouard Caron, an eminent lawyer and politician who became Lieutenant Governor of Quebec. Their son, Sir Adolphe Caron, who married Alice Bâby, daughter of the Honourable François Bâby, became the subsequent owner. The ewer was then passed down to their daughter Alice, who gave it to Mr and Mrs C. Anthony Law in 1942 as a wedding present. These last owners sold the ewer to Henry Birks in 1974.

46. NAC, Civil and Provincial Secretary, Lower Canada, RG 4 A 1, Series "S," 1760–1840, vol. 70, pp. 22279–82. "An Inventory of effects seized by the Sheriff of the District of Quebec to and for the use of His Majesty belonging to The Rev.d père Cazot [*sic*] ... ," 19 March 1800 (NAC reel C-3011).

47. Archives, Augustine Monastery of the Hôtel-Dieu de Québec, Quebec City. Annals (1877–88), 19 May 1881, pp. 166–67; 27 June 1881, p. 171.

48. NGC curatorial archives, letter from F. St George Spendlove to Charles Q. Ellis, 24 December 1947.

49. See Ward et al. 1980. For information on the silver collection in particular, see Buhler and Hood 1970.

50. Archives of American Art, Washington Center, Washington, D.C., Francis Patrick Garvan fonds, letter from E. Alfred Jones to Francis P. Garvan, 1 November 1929.

51. Ibid., 2 May 1926.

52. The inscription stamped on the edge of the small pedestal, *BERIAU PRETRE*, gives us the client's name, Abbé Louis-Michel Bériau (1728–1801); he presided over the Saint-Augustin-de-Desmaures parish, near Quebec City, from 1765 to 1801. Like Jacques Panet, priest at L'Islet during the same period, Bériau often commissioned work from François Ranvoyzé. It was well known that Panet was one of Ranvoyzé's regular clients, and for nearly half a century hired the sculptor to produce many sacred vessels and liturgical accessories, notably three famous gold vases that are now deposited at the Musée du Québec. During his time in Saint-Augustin, Abbé Bériau, for his part, had Ranvoyzé make not less than sixteen pieces, most of which still belong to the parish church.

53. In particular, Jones mentioned that he acquired a cup produced by the son of Ambroise Lafrance. This statement is the only indication that this son was a silversmith.

54. The drawings have the accession numbers 948.279.1–22. This collection, unique in the context of Quebec art, is divided into two subgroups. The first contains fifteen leaves with designs from the hand of Laurent Amiot; the watermarks have been dated to 1812, 1822, and 1827, and appear to indicate that the silversmith brought his portfolio up to date in those years. The seven other designs were done later and are perhaps the work of Ambroise Lafrance.

55. The silversmiths who executed the three ciboria have not been identified. The first was produced in Paris between 1687 and 1691, the second in Paris between 1750 and 1756, and the third in Liège between 1724 and 1763.

56. *Collections* 1965.

57. *Charles De Volpi* 1979.

58. NGC curatorial archives, letter from Henry G. Birks to F. Cleveland Morgan, 9 February 1940.

59. Ibid., letter from Henry G. Birks to Antoine Roy, 7 June 1949.

60. Ibid., letter from T.R. Macdonald to Henry G. Birks, 23 March 1955.

61. Ibid., "List of Articles Selected by Mr Louis Carrier, 7 June 1955, for Display in the Château Ramezay."

62. Ibid., letter from George MacBeath to Henry G. Birks, 27 January 1956.

63. Ibid., letter from Henry G. Birks to J.E. Cliver, 4 December 1964.

64. Ibid., typed list, 19 November 1975.

65. Ibid., letter from Guy Vadeboncoeur to Helen Graham, 30 April 1976.

66. Ibid., typed list, 1977.

67. Ibid., typed list, c. 19 January 1977.

68. Ibid., letter from Joseph Martin to Gérard Lavallée, 17 November 1983.

69. *Silver Thread* 1970.

70. *Newfoundland Historic Trust* 1971.

71. Bovey 1974.

72. Pichette and Vachon 1976.

73. Nanavati c. 1978.

74. Greenwood 1978.

75. Fox 1985.

76. NGC curatorial archives, letter from Henry G. Birks to John E. Langdon, 21 November 1966.

FORMAL AND DECORATIVE TENDENCIES IN QUEBEC SILVER

HOW DOES the development of Quebec silver relate to the major trends marking the history of the decorative arts in the Western world since the seventeenth century? Although other studies have examined the forms and ornamental elements characterizing silverwork in Quebec, the perspective has usually been documentary. Many articles have focussed on the lives and careers of silversmiths, and much attention has been paid to makers' marks. In fact, the most renowned publications in the field are those dealing with such marks. These studies, combined with archival research, make it possible to identify silversmiths and accurately date their work. Important as this is, it has limitations as a key to the evolution of Quebec silver. In the course of one career, for example, a silversmith may have worked in many different styles, variations explained neither by marks nor by archival sources. Stylistic analysis, on the other hand, can reliably verify the general tendencies distinguishing the forms and techniques employed by a particular artist or marking a given era. With a greater comprehension of these patterns, it is possible to discover the influences that came into play, and even determine the references or models used for a given work.

And yet, approaching the silver of Quebec by way of its stylistic history is a considerable challenge. Before attempting to use the concept of style to better understand the works in question, and more significantly, their formal evolution, we must define the term.

In silversmithing, as in the decorative arts in general, form is almost always determined essentially by function. Variations are therefore more often seen in ornamentation than in morphology, although certain forms and structures may be associated with specific eras. In the last few decades many studies, particularly on the history of architecture and the decorative arts, have addressed questions of typology. Making it possible to establish classification systems that operate at the level of types as well as genres, these studies have also helped cast light on styles – for although the notion of style is still being debated among art historians, definitions which allow it to be applied have long existed. Style may be perceived as an instrument of either generalization or singularization.[1] In the first case, it acts as a functional concept serving a body of knowledge whose main objective is to record and classify. In the second, it implies a degree of individual liberty in the way an overall aesthetic is applied, allowing artists to stamp their work with a "personal style." Theory about genres, and consequently styles, always hesitates between the two approaches. It becomes necessary to confront the system and the history to which the term is being applied to clarify a particular usage. Observing that style is "the constant form – and sometimes the constant elements, qualities, and expression – in the art of an individual or a group," Meyer Schapiro suggests it can therefore be used "as a criterion of the date and place of origin of works, and as a means of tracing relationships between schools of art....It is, besides, a common ground against which innovations and the individuality of particular works may be measured."[2] It is this last definition of style that we shall employ here.

A note of caution: when studying the decorative arts, we must distance ourselves considerably from the approaches usually taken in the field of visual arts, because the constants at work in establishing historical styles in the latter are not totally applicable to the former. The tendencies governing fine art since the Renaissance do not necessarily manifest themselves either according to the same terms or in the same fashion.

The Influence of Silver from France
Mannerism, Baroque, and Rococo

Imported silver and guild-trained immigrant silversmiths from France played an active part in the birth of the industry in Quebec, exercising a considerable influence from the mid-seventeenth right through to the late eighteenth centuries. This did not result in a monotonous uniformity of production, however:

quite the opposite. Based on works surviving from this time, three main stylistic tendencies marked the ornamentation and forms of silverwork in New France: the Mannerist, the Baroque, and the Rococo. The last two had the greatest effect on early Quebec silver.

In the seventeenth and eighteenth centuries, the French-Canadian aristocracy and clergy were the silversmiths' major clients. Along with domestic articles, we find numerous sacred vessels used in Roman Catholic worship, some imported from France and others made locally. Mannerist-inspired pieces are rare, and, sadly, none are to be found at the National Gallery of Canada. Only some long-established monasteries in Quebec City have the good fortune to own works associated with this trend, all brought from the home country around 1650.

Several pieces in the National Gallery's collection provide an insight into the Baroque style as expressed in this country, however. The small *Chalice* (NGC 16872) made in 1704 by the Paris silversmith Jean-Baptiste Loir (active 1689–1716) is highly architectural. The cup and foot are treated minimally, the only ornamentation being the alternating egg-shaped *ovoli* and leaves around the base. The inside edge of the frieze is beaded. The knop (knob or bulb), more ornate, is flanked by two collar knops serving as amortizements (sloping supports). Its upper section is decorated with a gadrooned frieze (one with long, convex, parallel lobes or bosses), and its lower portion with foliage. Similar characteristics appear in the magnificent *Ciborium* (see fig. 9) produced in the colony slightly later by the Quebec silversmith Jacques Pagé, *dit* Quercy. Pagé was apprenticed to Michel Levasseur, a French silversmith who practised his trade in New France between 1700 and 1710 or so. The ciborium's most striking feature is its pure, well-defined form. The diameter of the foot is slightly greater than that of the cup, creating visual stability. The ornamentation is subdued: the moulding of the foot is decorated with stylized acanthus leaves, the crown of the knop is highlighted by a frieze of narrow, straight gadroons, and the cup displays a subtle, pulsating effect due to planishing (slight smoothing of the surface with a convex hammer). The finial (terminal ornament on the lid) supporting a cross imparts verticality to the work.

Domestic silver of the period, produced by the same artists, shows a similar architectural tendency. Contemporary silversmiths in France developed specialties, but those in New France accepted commissions indiscriminately from both the Church and aristocracy. The "ecuelle," a bowl with flat handles used for serving soups of meats and vegetables cooked together in a pot, maintained its popularity throughout the eighteenth century. Ecuelles were produced by numerous silversmiths, including Roland Paradis (c. 1696–1754), born in Paris, who established a workshop in New France around 1728. He made, for example, the *Ecuelle with the Arms of the Le Ber de Senneville and Gaultier de la Vérendry Families* (NGC 24128), which typified mid-eighteenth-century taste.[3] The work's most imposing feature is the body's round, sturdy form. It is equipped with two large ears cut from a flat piece of silver, which are placed symmetrically near the rim. The sober ornamentation, consisting of splayed palmettes on the ears and engraved coats of arms centred on one side, softens the stoutness of the piece.

Another maker whose works embody the Baroque spirit and who contributed to its popularity is Paul Lambert, *dit* Saint-Paul. The *Plate with the Monogram of the Duperron Bâby Family* (see fig. 12) may have been an ecuelle tray. Its strength lies in the fullness of its forms, brought out by five lobes making up the rim. Although this model of plate was extremely popular in the eighteenth century, Lambert's is the only example produced in New France that has been discovered to date. French imports helped make them fashionable in the colony, however. One such is the *Plate with the Coat of Arms of the Bâby Family* (fig. 19) made by Michel Delapierre (active c. 1737–1785). Occasional surviving inventories reveal that the tables of prominent families were usually graced by both imported silver and articles produced locally.

Lambert also made liturgical silver, the work for which he is best known.[4] His exquisite *Censer* (fig. 20) produced in 1746 for the Saint-Pierre parish on Île-d'Orléans displays an architectural character overall, but numerous embossed and engraved motifs occupy nearly all the available surfaces. The ornamentation, replete with acanthus leaves and cherub heads, is in the Louis XIV style. It acts to accentuate the forms; the scale of the motifs is always in proportion to the surfaces they ornament. Each section of the paunch, for example, is highlighted by a different motif: the more protruding part features three large cherub heads located under the cylinders holding the chains fastened to the chimney cover and interspersed with bouquets of flowers. The lower part is decorated with water leaves and stylized acanthus leaves alternating on a matte ground. The result is rich and imposing.

The *Altar Candlestick* (see fig. 8) by the same silversmith is similar in approach. It was commissioned to form a pair with a seventeenth-century Parisian candlestick owned by the Saint-Nicolas parish.[5] Although its form matches that of its French counterpart, Lambert's candlestick is distinguished by its motifs, which nonetheless reflect the same Baroque spirit. The stylized water-leaf frieze following the entire moulding of the base and, in particular, the large, formalized acanthus leaves on a matte ground which adorn the lower portion of the knop, are trademarks of the artist.

The infatuation with the Baroque aesthetic was so great that its popularity lasted until around 1785 and even beyond, especially in liturgical silver (although other influences were emerging, as we will soon see). The demands of clients, notably certain parish priests, played a part in this. Among silversmiths, François Ranvoyzé (1739–1819), by virtue of his enthusiasm for the Baroque, must be credited more than anyone else with prolonging it as a style.[6] Born in Quebec City during the French regime, he trained under Ignace-François Delezenne (1718–1790), a brilliant silversmith from Lille, who immigrated to New France around 1740.[7] Delezenne's surviving work shows us that Ranvoyzé must have

Fig. 19
Michel Delapierre
Active Paris c. 1737–1785
Plate with the Coat of Arms of the Bâby Family c. 1749–50
Silver
NGC, purchased 1994 (37518)

been exposed to the art of the Ancien Régime very early. In addition, the thinness of the metal Ranvoyzé employed, as well as his particular openwork technique, suggest that he must have produced silver ornaments used for barter in the fur trade with Amerindian trappers in the course of his apprenticeship.

However, Ranvoyzé soon added his personal touch to the skills acquired from his master. Two domestic pieces made in the first decade after opening his workshop clearly reveal his artistic leanings. The large baluster-shaped *Ewer of François Ranvoyzé* (see fig. 14), which he made for his personal and family use, displays the formal qualities of many French ewers dating from the first half of the eighteenth century. The paunch rests on a base with a cyma recta moulding (a moulding that is concave above and convex below), decorated with a frieze of twisted gadroons.

Fig. 20
Paul Lambert, *dit* Saint-Paul
Arras, France 1691? – Quebec City 1749
Censer 1746
Silver
NGC, Gift of the Henry Birks Collection of Canadian
Silver, 1979 (27771)

The vessel is encircled by three mouldings: the first is on the pear-shaped paunch, the second is at the start of the neck, and the third, wider than the others, is just below the hinged lid. The spout is in the form of a woman's mask; she is wearing a ruff around her neck and a large plumed hat. The handle consists of a series of volutes (scrolled shapes), and the cyma recta moulding gives a convex form to the lid, which features a scrolled thumb-piece, a turned-bud finial in the centre, and a gadrooned top. Finally, just below the spout between the middle and lower mouldings on the paunch, we see a large engraved cartouche (decorative frame for inscriptions, initials, etc.) resembling a coat of arms surmounted by a crown and displaying the doubled monogram *FR*. Ranvoyzé appears to have been inspired by some older French ewer: the work bears many similarities to the one made in Paris by Éloi Guérin in 1728–29 and now at the Quebec archdiocese, as well as to the *Ewer with the Arms of the Sabrevois de Bleury Family* produced by Gabriel Viaucourt (accredited Paris, 1698–after 1749) in 1739–40 and now at the Basilica of Notre-Dame de Montréal in Montreal. This is not surprising since every surviving Ranvoyzé ewer, whether domestic or baptismal, refers to a Parisian model of the late seventeenth or early eighteenth centuries.[8]

The *Multilobed Plate* (NGC 38079) he produced around the same time (c. 1771–81) is also of considerable interest. In this exquisite interpretation, the silversmith has strayed considerably from the norm, streamlining the contours and emphasizing the shape of the lobes. The source is recognizable, but the freedom of the adaptation allows us to describe it as a new creation. This is a departure. Ranvoyzé did not generally make innovations in form, but rather appropriated the vocabulary of the late seventeenth and early eighteenth centuries. His true contribution lay in the field of decoration.

From about 1782, Ranvoyzé began to ornament his work in a new style that nonetheless remained thoroughly Baroque in spirit.[9] It is exemplified by his unique *Ecuelle Cover* (NGC 24127.2) from about the same time. The surface is decorated with flowers, foliage, and large exotic fruit, broadly treated and arranged asymmetrically in a dynamic composition. The motifs completely cover the centrally located knob and are then channelled into two friezes, both in perfect harmony with the cover's basic form. In designing this pattern, Ranvoyzé was undoubtedly inspired by the friezes with engraved plant-like and floral motifs found on many Neo-Classical British vessels and vases from the same period, adapting the scale and rendering them in an entirely new manner.[10] He produced a number of variations, some using mainly foliage, others mostly flowers and fruit.

Whatever the motifs, Ranvoyzé generally placed them in a frieze designed, as on the *Ecuelle Cover*, to respect the object's basic form. For example, the *Aspersorium* (fig. 21) he made in 1798 for the Saint-Pierre parish on Île-d'Orléans displays two distinct friezes, separated by a polished band, that respectively highlight the curve and countercurve of the paunch – a treatment that emphasizes the monumental character of the piece despite its limited size. Within the frieze, the

artist was inventive, softening his approach as appropriate. In his *Chalice* (NGC 24016) of 1784, for example, although chased acanthus leaves form a frieze around the base moulding of the foot, other characteristic motifs cover the rest of the dome and nimbly envelop the oval knop on the stem and the calyx (applied decoration encircling the lower part of the cup). The influence of Ranvoyzé's original technique broadened the scope of the Baroque style, allowing the movement to persist into the late eighteenth century.

While the Baroque had a strong impact on silver produced in the eighteenth century, other movements left their mark as well, notably Rococo. The Rococo

Fig. 22
Guillaume Loir
Paris c. 1694–1769
Monstrance 1750
Silver, gold, and crystal
NGC, purchased 1975 (18437)

style was present in New France due to articles imported from Paris workshops. Much less constrained by architectural principles, Rococo is characterized by supple, curved forms, asymmetry, and the presence of rocaille elements (fancy rock-, shell-, floral-, foliage-, and scrollwork) and C-shaped and S-shaped motifs. The large *Monstrance* (fig. 22) by Guillaume Loir (c. 1694–1769), presented by the intendant François Bigot to the Saint-Pierre parish on Île-d'Orléans on 4 October 1750 is an eloquent testimony to this style.[11] Granted that the baluster-like form and symmetrical ornamentation herald the imminent rise of Neo-Classicism, the top of the base, which is covered with volutes and even with a large rocaille cartouche placed centrally to the rear, speaks to the work's Rococo orientation. The lower portion of the knop and the upper section of the collar knop are decorated with twisted fluting. The rays of the sun, though symmetrically arranged, are treated freely enough to lend fluidity and movement to the work.

A *Ciborium* (NGC 18180) made in Paris in 1756–57 by Alexis Porcher (active 1725–1781) contains Rococo elements in the calyx, whose ornamentation consists of applied motifs. A series of interlaced and elongated C-shaped forms enclose cascades of foliage alternating with seashells. A motif composed of a flute surmounted by an ovum links the interlace and ties the piece rhythmically together. The use of applied motifs allowed the silversmith to fully develop the Rococo character of this work.

Neo-Classicism

In September of 1759, Quebec City, the capital of New France, fell to the English army, and in 1763, after several years of military rule, the Treaty of Paris made the transfer of power official. Shortly after that, in 1775, the Americans took control of Montreal and besieged Quebec City. They were repelled, going on to declare an independent United States of America in 1776. Finally, in 1791, the Constitutional Act divided the territory into Upper and Lower Canada and created a governor, legislative council, and legislative assembly for each. For the first time since the English Conquest, the official right of the francophone majority in Lower Canada to decide its destiny was recognized by statute. Thus, owing to politics, war, and mere chance, the area that was known as New France in 1759 became, by 1791, one of the sole remaining British territories in North America.

These political transformations were soon accompanied by important demographic changes. The population of the capital, Quebec City, rose from 3,497 in 1762 to 15,839 in 1818, becoming more diversified as well.[12] In the summer of 1795, two-thirds of all residents were "Canadiens", or francophones, and one third anglophones, but by 1818 the proportions had stabilized at sixty per cent francophone and forty per cent anglophone – a result of the waves of British immigration occurring since the Conquest.[13] The population increase, combined with greater demographic diversity, upset the colony's entire economic structure. The role of Quebec

City, the country's only inland seaport, was changed by the appearance of merchants in large numbers; a certain kind of "luxury" was now within reach of an constantly increasing number of residents, who formed an emerging middle class.

Gradually, the Quebec life-style was also transformed, particularly in regard to living space. Under the French regime homes tended to be small, with few rooms, generally limited to one bedroom and one other room which served all other purposes. In the late eighteenth century not only did the number of rooms significantly increase but a precise function became attached to each.[14] This gave rise to a substantial expansion in both the amount and kind of furniture and domestic objects used.[15] The dining room, for example, made its appearance in the late eighteenth century,[16] creating a demand for both new types of furniture and new objects conceived especially for this purpose.

How was silver affected by these profound changes? It is revealing to compare the typology of domestic pieces seen during the French regime with those in use by 1800. In New France, the most usual types of domestic articles were few in number: spoons, ragoût spoons, forks, beakers, wine tasters, and ecuelles. More rarely, plates with scalloped rims, gadrooned fruit bowls, and ewers were to be found. Certain objects were apparently so rare that they seem to have been the exclusive privilege of dignitaries and the wealthy, and are known today only through documentation: olive spoons, salad bowls, coffee pots, sauce-boats, oil cruets, sugar bowls, and egg cups. By 1800, cutlery had become more specialized. Now there were not merely forks, but dining forks, salad forks, and dessert forks. The types of spoons and ladles increased as well. Gradually, christening mugs, sugar tongs, and snuff boxes made their appearance. The introduction of tea-drinking led to the import and local production of teapots and tea caddies, soon followed by sugar bowls and milk jugs, which were generally made individually but occasionally produced as a tea set. Salt cellars, nutcrackers, kidney brochettes, and wine funnels rounded out the panoply of tableware, attesting to an evolution in the art of dining. Though less common, ewers, soup tureens, coffee pots, cake baskets, saucepans, oil cruets, mustard pots, pap-boats, and tea trays were also to be found, to name the principal objects.

The stronger economy had a similar effect on liturgical silver. Under the French regime, except for the one cathedral in Quebec City and a few religious communities, churches appear to have possessed very modest silver collections, often limited to the essential sacred vessels: chalice and paten, ciborium, and monstrance. It was not unusual for the monstrance and ciborium to share the same foot. There were even cases in which the parish had to settle for a monstrance in gilded wood.[17] Some sacristies housed a silver censer, silver collection plate, and occasionally silver altar cruets but in most instances, these vessels were made of pewter, copper, or brass.

Around 1800, the situation changed somewhat. The chalice, paten, ciborium, and monstrance were still present but it became increasingly common to find an

Fig. 23
John Robins
Active London, England, 1771–1831
Pair of Sauce Tureens and Matching Trays with Monogram of the Duperron Bâby Family 1782–83
Silver
NGC, Bequest of Louis de la Chesnaye Audette, O.C., Q.C., Ottawa, 1996, in memory of Judge and
Mme Arthur Audette (38280.1–6)

aspersorium, censer, incense boat, and baptismal ewer, sometimes presented on a tray, as well as matching altar cruets and their tray, and ampullae containing holy oil, often with a matching box. Paxes, piscinae, acolytes' candlesticks, sanctuary lamps, and processional crosses were also in common use at the time; reliquaries, altar crosses, and statues were commissioned, although rarely. On both the domestic and religious fronts, the silversmithing industry was shaken by the introduction of new ideas and practices. From a formal and decorative perspective, these innovations bore the mark of Neo-Classicism.

Appearing in the last third of the eighteenth century, Neo-Classicism acted as something of an opposing force to the artificiality and decorative excesses of Rococo. In France, it was known by various names, depending on the period: Louis XVI, Directoire, Empire, and Charles X. In England, the style emerged during the long reign of George III, and may be divided into three periods known as Early Georgian, Late Georgian, and Regency. Neo-Classicism imposed a severity of line and form on silverwork, as it did on other art forms. The style was seen in Canada from the 1770s to about 1830, a fascinating period in the history of Quebec silver. This era not only produced Quebec's finest silversmiths but also marked the convergence of the established silversmithing tradition based in the Baroque and Rococo with the new French and British Neo-Classical influences. The interplay between them all was pivotal to the artistic activity of the era, in which various forms of expression flourished side by side, often boldly coexisting within the same art work.

Fig. 24
Sheffield?, England, 1780–1800
Salt Dish from the Breakey Family
Silver plate on copper (Sheffield plate)
Private collection

While some immigrants to Canada brought silver with them, it soon became more common to import it from Britain. The *Pair of Sauce Tureens and Matching Trays with Monogram of the Duperron Bâby Family* (fig. 23) made in London in 1782–83 by John Robins (active 1771–1831) exemplifies the new aesthetic. Genuine prototypes of English Neo-Classicism, these sauce tureens and trays illustrate the sobriety of the style and its contrast with Rococo. Resting on an oval base, the body of each tureen is in the form of an elongated skiff. The elegantly curved handle echoes its overall shape. The diamond-shaped tray features a beaded border; festoons of engraved foliage ornament the inside edge. The rim of the base and upper edge of the tureen display the same beading, and its lid presents a similarly undulating effect; the handle is in the form of a bud garnished with beads. This pair of Adam-style sauce tureens has an interesting provenance: acquired by Jacques Bâby, *dit* Duperron, sometime between 1782 and 1789,[18] they were later appraised by Ranvoyzé when an inventory was taken of Bâby's estate in 1800.[19] The rise of the new style was reflected not only in solid-silver articles, but in pieces of pewter, porcelain, and Sheffield plate (see fig. 24).[20]

Imports remained popular, serving to keep local patrons and silversmiths informed about stylistic developments on the other side of the Atlantic. For example, James Leslie (1786–1873), a Montreal merchant and politician of Scots origin, acquired an enormous set of silver tableware several years after his marriage, which took place in 1815. Made in London, it included a *Tea Set* (NGC 24017.1–3) made in 1818–19 by the Englishman Charles Price (accredited 1797–after 1826).[21] The spherical form of the teapot is typical of the Regency style. The paunch and top of the lid are gadrooned, and the handle and spout are decorated with acanthus leaves.

Among the imports were pieces offered as gifts or tributes; the most imposing of these were made in England. Without question, a large Communion set based on designs by Jean-Jacques Boileau (n.d.) and made by Philip Cornman (active London, England, before 1793–after 1807) and Joseph Preddy (accredited London, England 1773–after 1803) for Rundell and Bridge in 1802–03 was the most prestigious and significant work of this kind to arrive in Quebec at the time. It was a gift from George III to the Anglican cathedral in Quebec City.[22] This exceptional set, which helped to inspire lasting enthusiasm for the Georgian style in Quebec City, is still housed in the cathedral.

It was quite usual for a gift from the reigning monarch to be produced in London and then sent overseas with the purpose of consolidating the royal reputation in the colonies. Similarly, in 1832, when the citizens of Quebec City wanted to show their gratitude to John Neilson for having successfully pleaded their case before the Crown in 1823 and 1828, they too looked towards the British capital. The large, krater-shaped, historiated *Cup Presented to John Neilson* (fig. 25) at a banquet on 4 January 1832 is the work of the London silversmith Joseph Craddock (active 1806–after 1831). The sides are decorated with an unusual series of four scenes highlighting the recipient's political achievements. On the front is the delegation, made up of Neilson, who is kneeling, backed by Denis-Benjamin Viger and Augustin Cuviller; he is presenting their request to George IV, seated on his throne with a courtier on either side. On the other side, two allegorical figures framed by branches of laurel draw attention to the inscription:

À John Neilson, écuyer, M.P.P., député deux fois auprès du Parlement impérial pour défendre les droits des Canadiens. Ce léger tribut de reconnaissance lui est offert en mémoire des services qu'il a rendus au pays, et comme hommage à ses vertus civiques. Québec, 1831

(To John Neilson, Esquire, M.P.P., deputized twice to the Imperial Parliament to defend the rights of Canadians. We offer him this small tribute of recognition in memory of the services which he has rendered to the country, and as homage to his civic virtues. Quebec City, 1831)

Fig. 25
Joseph Craddock
Active London, England 1806 – after 1831
Cup Presented to John Neilson 1831
Silver
Musée du Québec, Quebec City (84.21)

One of the sides features a soldier tearing up the Quebec Act and offering its symbolic chains to Canada, which is protected by the British lion and by an allegorical figure positioned between the soldier and the spirit of Lower Canada. On the fourth side, Cincinnatus abandons his plough to assume his role as dictator. It is regrettable that the details of the story behind the commissioning of this cup have not yet been pieced together: local artists must have been involved in its conception, if only to provide the drawings used as the basis for the scenes on the plinth, which depict the Neilson house, a horse-drawn sleigh loaded with wood, an Amerindian family, and a bark canoe.[23]

A large *Ewer* (fig. 26) was presented by the merchants of Quebec City and Montreal, probably in 1832, to Captain John Neill, whose brig, the *Sophia*, made the crossing between Greenock and Quebec City three times during the 1831 shipping season. Its ovoid paunch, along with motifs representing vine leaves, bunches of grapes, water leaves, and even a shell on the lid, alluding to the sea, clearly mark it as Regency in style. London was a fertile and popular source for such presentation pieces, which ranged from illustrious works like the royal gift described above to more modest objects made and engraved in advance according to a standard formula. They played a key role in establishing and cultivating a taste for English silver in Canada.

Although high-quality imports arrived in the country through different channels at various times, they were not the only means by which the Regency style was disseminated. Several silversmiths immigrated to Lower Canada from the British Isles during this period. The career of James G. Hanna (c. 1737–1806) is typical of the new type of practice that was being set up in Quebec City shortly after 1760. An Irishman who moved to Quebec City in 1763 or 1764, Hanna owned a shop called the Eagle and Watch. Known primarily as a silversmith, he was also a clock- and watchmaker and a merchant. Jewellery, silver tableware, weapons, scientific instruments, and a variety of other objects were carefully listed in advertisements he placed in the capital's newspapers.[24] There is every indication that Hanna, and others like him, imported most of the articles they sold from the United Kingdom, but also produced utensils and other small objects, often in partnership with silversmiths who had already set up shop in Canada, at least wherever such local artisans were available. This explains the existence of pieces bearing two marks, for example, those of James Orkney (1760–1832), who was Hanna's son-in-law, and of the silversmith Joseph Sasseville (1790–1837).[25]

In addition to these contributions, significant but having only a modest impact from an artistic point of view, there were more powerful sources of renewal and change. Robert Cruickshank (c. 1748–1809), of Scottish origin, was in the forefront.[26] Arriving in Montreal by 1773, he set up a full-fledged business, soon taking on journeymen and apprentices and turning out a high volume of pieces for use in the fur trade while accepting commissions from the Roman Catholic Church, the aristocracy, and the bourgeoisie. Although he aggressively pursued several

Fig. 26
London, England, nineteenth century
Ewer Presented to Captain John Neill 1832
Silver
Private collection

activities at the same time, Cruickshank was a practising silversmith throughout his career and his work displays a great deal of homogeneity attributable to his espousal of Neo-Classicism, particularly the style of Robert Adam.

Cruickshank's *Tea Set with the Monogram of the Chartier de Lotbinière Family* (fig. 27), one of the oldest surviving sets produced in Canada, is a remarkable testament to his contribution. The teapot and stand, sugar bowl, and milk jug are a

vivid evocation of their era: fluid lines and clean contours place them unmistakably in the last decade of the eighteenth century. In fact, Cruickshank had so thoroughly mastered the elements of the Late Georgian style that he was able to interpret it with great individuality. The teapot's moulded foot ring and double shoulder represent departures from the basic style, as does the sturdiness of the sugar bowl. The milk jug is distinguished for being a miniature version of the large wine ewers produced at this time. The set's ornamentation consists of little more than the sheen of the polished metal, except for the family monogram, surmounted by an earl's coronet, which is engraved on each piece, making them somewhat less austere. In subsequent works, Cruickshank adorned the edges of his vessels with delicate, meticulously engraved friezes.

Several years before the creation of the Chartier de Lotbinière tea set, when he was working with Michael Arnoldi, Cruickshank had produced an extraordinary set of *Altar Cruets* (NGC 27776.1–2), also modelled after large English wine ewers, although without handles. They are examples of the subtle exchange between the domestic and religious that gave rise to new forms in Quebec liturgical silver. While the shapes and ornamentation of cruets produced during the previous era tended towards complication, pure forms like these, with little decoration, became popular within a very short time.

There has been much speculation about the career of Pierre Huguet, *dit* Latour (1749–1817), one of Cruickshank's contemporaries. He appears to have been a dealer in silver rather than a practising silversmith. In 1781, describing himself as a wig maker, Huguet signed a one-year contract with Simon Beauregard (n.d.), a twenty-one-year-old silversmith, stipulating that the young apprentice was to make as many pendant earrings as possible.[27] That same year he reached a similar agreement with François Larsonneur (1762–1806).[28] In both cases, Huguet appears to have acted as a merchant or dealer, ordering silver pieces such as brooches or hair ornaments for use in the fur trade (fig. 28). Note that, four years later on 21 August 1785, when he hired Michel Létourneau (?–1797) as an apprentice, the contract specified that the young man was to learn his craft from Huguet "or his representatives."[29] This suggests that Huguet was indeed a merchant who had been in the habit of purchasing trade silver from independent silversmiths, and who suddenly decided to set up his own business, which he operated like any other commercial enterprise, without necessarily wielding a hammer himself. He was a gifted organizer rather than a truly creative force, and in this sense his workshop was a harbinger of the industrial age, as were the activities of the contemporary Montreal sculptor Louis Quévillon (1749–1823).[30] As a result, his commercial activities expanded over the years.

It was not until 1794 that Huguet made a modest entry into the market for liturgical silver by doing some repairs on sacred vessels belonging to the church of Notre-Dame de Montréal.[31] Almost ten years passed before his workshop filled its first church order in 1803, an event that appears to have coincided with the entry into the shop of an as-yet-unidentified silversmith with expertise in this area.[32] Huguet moved his firm to a new stone building the same year.[33] By deduction, it would seem that 1803 was also the year in which he began to produce a significant amount of domestic silver. Whatever the details, however, the body of work associated with Huguet provides ample evidence of the ascendancy of British Neo-Classicism.

A particularly beautiful example of this style is a large, oblong *Sauce-boat* (see fig. 13) set on three feet. This design, successor to the rocaille style, with its straight, moulded edges and handle forming opposing curves, echoes works produced by London silversmiths in about 1815. The unusually thick metal makes this piece even sturdier than its European counterparts.

Liturgical articles from the Huguet workshop reveal the same aesthetic concerns, though it was obviously more difficult to find appropriate British models

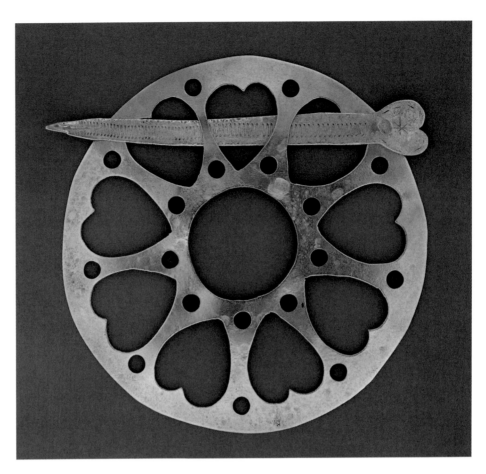

Fig. 28
Robert Cruikshank
Aberdeen c. 1748 – at sea, 1809
Hair Ornament between 1773 and 1809
NGC, Gift of the Henry Birks Collection of Canadian Silver, 1979 (27743.49)

for Roman Catholic religious silver. It was the approach rather than the actual designs that served as inspiration, as in a Huguet *Ciborium* (NGC 27874) that has little in common with works produced by silversmiths like Ranvoyzé just a short time earlier. The most striking features of this vessel, the source of its power and character, are its pure lines and harmonious proportions. To create greater visual stability, the diameter of the foot is a bit greater than that of the cup. A slight bulge in the dome of the foot creates an upward movement echoing that of the lid. The silversmith employs a minimum of chasing, choosing instead to emphasize the large polished surfaces. Chasing is found only in specific areas including the knop, the two adjacent collar knops and the frieze around the moulding on the foot. Limiting the motifs to a variety of gadroons contributes to the work's unity and monumentality, two basic Neo-Classical principles.

Fig. 29
Pierre Huguet, *dit* Latour
Quebec City 1749 – Montreal 1817
Aspersorium c. 1803–17
Silver
NGC, Gift of the Henry Birks Collection of Canadian Silver, 1979 (27831)

Although the inverted-pear shape of the paunch on the *Aspersorium* (fig. 29; also known as a Holy Water stoup) by Huguet recalls Rococo, the polished surfaces and ornamentation indicate a further shift towards Neo-Classicism. The smooth sections of the basin have been given a flawless sheen which reflects light, the moulding on the foot is highlighted by a frieze of rather wide, simple gadroons, which make the base appear more monumental, and the bulge is decorated with festoons of laurel leaves, a favourite Neo-Classical motif. In an original treatment, the ornamentation is flat and linear, recalling friezes engraved on contemporary domestic objects. Such innovations played a significant role in updating the style of liturgical silver, especially in the Montreal area.

73

Fig. 30
Salomon Marion
Lachenaie, Quebec 1782 – Montreal 1830
Pair of Salt Dishes c. 1815–30
Silver, gold, and crystal
NGC, Gift of the Henry Birks Collection of Canadian Silver, 1979 (25265.1–2)

This approach would come to be adopted by most other Quebec silversmiths active at this time. Trained at the Huguet workshop,[34] Salomon Marion remained there after his apprenticeship.[35] During his brief personal career, which barely covered the years 1815 through 1830, he produced an impressive body of work, including several masterpieces of Quebec silver. Among his creations is a *Pair of Salt Dishes* (fig. 30) quite remarkable for the period. The cut-glass vessels are mounted on gilt silver disks with gadrooned rims – a design and motifs recalling works made in London around 1800. His *Montreal Agricultural Society Cup* (see fig. 15), awarded to Robert Gillespie in 1820, is one of the earliest presentation pieces made in the country; like the salt dishes, its shape recalls silver produced in London two decades earlier. It is distinguished, however, by the presence of a lower cup encased in a calyx ornamented with an array of leaves and surrounded by a delicately chased frieze. The polished area for the inscription on the upper part of the cup is flanked by engravings of a harrow and a ploughshare.

Marion also created a *Tea Set with the Arms of the Coffin Family* (NGC 24011.1–4), which includes a teapot, a hot-water pot – today deprived of its stand – a sugar bowl, and a milk jug. The forms are simple, circular, and compressed. The teapot is a sphere supported by a foot and divided by horizontal moulding; the otherwise stout vessel is lightened by the graceful curves of its handle and spout, an effect enhanced by a skilfully curved lid. Highly polished metal gives the work a quasi-

Fig. 31
Salomon Marion
Lachenaie, Quebec 1782 – Montreal 1830
Tea Set c. 1815–30
Silver, gold, and ivory
NGC, Gift of the Henry Birks Collection of Canadian Silver, 1979 (27786.1–3)

architectural character – also evident in the sugar bowl and milk jug, whose chased ornamentation is limited to acanthus leaves that highlight the handles.

Created during the same period, another Marion *Tea Set* (fig. 31) demonstrates a different aspect of British Neo-Classicism while attesting to the versatility of the artist. This interpretation of the Regency style makes use of full forms, a rectangular design, and a decoration of the wide gadroons which would become a standard Neo-Classical motif. The artist's use of thin metal confirms that technical advances were being made. In England, remarkably thin silver leaf prepared in rolling sheets had been in common use since the late eighteenth century. Cruickshank had employed similar sheets in Montreal and other artisans may also have had access to this material. In fact, they may have been so eager to incorporate it into their work that they made the required leaf themselves, hammering it by hand.

Fig. 32
Salomon Marion
Lachenaie, Quebec 1782 – Montreal 1830
Aspersorium 1825
Silver
NGC, Gift of the Henry Birks Collection of Canadian Silver, 1979 (24020)

Even the liturgical articles Marion produced bear the imprint of British Neo-Classicism. For example, the paunch of his portable *Aspersorium* (fig. 32) dating from 1825 is obviously modelled on the inverted-pear shape he had mastered during his years in the Huguet workshop. This shape served as the basis for most of the aspersoriums created in the Montreal region during the first quarter of the nineteenth century. The idea of adorning the bulge of the paunch with festoons was introduced in the late eighteenth century by Laurent Amiot, as we will soon see. While most of the works from the Huguet workshop can be described as Adamesque, here the sumptuous acanthus leaves on the upper portion of the receptacle combine with the foliage at the intersection of the paunch and foot to convey a distinctive Regency feel.

In addition to the well-established silversmiths, there were several other active craftsmen whose activities are not as well documented but whose surviving works show that they, too, played a determining role in the evolution of Canadian Neo-Classicism. Some were retailers who stamped their mark on pieces by other makers, while carrying on modest personal careers. James Smillie, Jr. (1807–1885), was one such retailer. He probably stamped a *Mustard Pot and Spoon* (NGC 3768.1–2) in that context. A well-known engraver who emigrated from Scotland to Quebec City in 1828, Smillie does not appear to have worked as a silversmith.[36] However, he may have done engraving for some of them and thus developed an interest in the craft. The cylindrical mustard pot features openwork sides that allow the blue-crystal lining to show through. Engraving in the form of festoons, along with a handle shaped like a question mark, are direct references to the silver of late-eighteenth-century London.

Whereas Smillie worked in Quebec City, Nelson Walker (1799–after 1885) was based in Montreal, where he is thought to have set up shop by 1826 and remained in business until his return to Great Britain in 1855.[37] He may well have continued to procure supplies for his retail business from England. Walker advertised himself as an engraver, a jeweller, and a clock-maker, but his mark is most often found on tableware. The large *Beaker of Captain John Neill* (NGC 24118) was presented to the captain by the passengers on the ship *Robertson* in September 1834, after their arrival in Montreal.[38] A simple piece with curved contours, it is trimmed with a moulded lip and footband. The ornamentation consists of a gilt-lined interior and a lengthy inscription, which recounts the circumstances under which the gift was presented. The work incorporates the principles which had brought Neo-Classicism into favour and which, as we shall see in the next section, knew a second revival after 1830.

Despite the significant contribution made by Robert Cruickshank and the dynamic innovations introduced by Pierre Huguet, it was the personality of Laurent Amiot that dominated this entire period. His was an interesting history. Apparently aware that the artistic milieu was somewhat outdated, and wishing to promote the development of a French-Canadian intellectual elite after the British Conquest, the Roman Catholic Church had earlier helped send another artist of seminal importance, François Baillairgé (1759–1830), to study in France between 1778 to 1781. Despite the shortness of his stay, Baillairgé was able to pursue his training in a rich and stimulating environment, which in turn allowed him to play a major role in reviving the arts of painting, sculpture, and even architecture in the new world.[39] The success of this initiative encouraged the same authorities to arrange a Parisian sojourn for a promising silversmith the next year, Laurent Amiot.

Amiot had learned the rudiments of his craft in the workshop of his brother, the silversmith Jean-Nicolas Amiot (1750–1821), before leaving for France in 1782. Younger than Baillairgé at the time of his departure, Amiot remained in Europe for five years rather than three. Unfortunately, the identity of the master who oversaw Amiot's training and the name of the workshop remain a mystery, but he probably studied in a non-guild workshop in Paris. When he returned to Quebec in the spring of 1787, armed with a high degree of technical expertise, Amiot was well prepared to disseminate the Louis XVI style then popular in Paris.[40]

Several documents attest to Amiot's high regard for silversmithing and its practitioners. In 1816, he instructed a notary to refer to him as a "Maître es Art Orfèvre" (master of the silversmithing art).[41] Twenty years later, in another similar circumstance, he had the word "métier" (craft) replaced with the phrase "Art d'Orfèvrerie" (art of silversmithing). Clearly, he was conscious of his status as a creator.[42] Although silversmiths like Cruickshank, and especially Huguet, tended to turn the trade into an industry, Amiot insisted that his work be viewed as art and silversmiths as artists not artisans.

Amiot is of particular interest for a related, noteworthy reason. Like the master Parisian silversmiths of the period who adhered to the finest academic traditions, but unlike his peers, he made preliminary sketches in preparation for his works. Among the Quebec silversmiths active before 1925, Amiot is the only one for whom we have a collection of drawings. Dating from about 1825, the series appears to be an updated version of his portfolio; it contains designs of basic models intended for his ecclesiastical clientele. These afford a unique glimpse of both his creative process and the era. Today, most are housed at the Royal Ontario Museum.

With designs like these, which promulgated an aesthetic based on the Louis XVI style, Amiot initiated a genuine revival. This is quite evident in the silver he produced for both the table and the altar. The large *Ewer* (see fig. 4) at the National Gallery of Canada is among his most accomplished works. It rests on a circular foot enveloped by a cyma recta and a delicate roundel ornamented with stylized laurels. The urn-shaped paunch sits directly on top of this foot; the lower section of the paunch is adorned with a corolla of formalized water leaves and the protruding portion by a frieze of laurels in full bloom. The smooth neck emerges in a graceful, semicircular curve from a beaded frieze; its lip is ornamented with laurels, as is the convex, hinged lid. The bud finial at the centre of the lid is surrounded by rayed water leaves. The handle, in the form of a ribboned volute, is attached by circles of acanthus leaves. A comparison of this work with the *Ewer of François Ranvoyzé* (see fig. 14) created just a few years earlier demonstrates the modernity of Amiot's ideas.

The sumptuous *Chalice* (fig. 33) commissioned by the Saint-Cuthbert parish in 1812 shows another of Amiot's innovations. The most striking feature is its height: 31.75 centimetres. The artist makes his presence felt through his mastery

Fig. 33
Laurent Amiot
Quebec City 1764–1839
Chalice 1812
Silver and gold
NGC, Gift of the Henry Birks Collection of Canadian Silver, 1979 (27739)

Fig. 34
Laurent Amiot
Quebec City 1764–1839
Cup c. 1825
Silver
NGC, purchased 1990 (30574)

of the art of composition, skilfully combining the various components so the ornaments complement the surfaces they decorate. The large foot is embellished with an imposing ogee (S-shaped) moulding, divided into four rectilinear panels with matte edges that alternate with an equal number of oblong rosettes. A torus ornamented with stylized laurels defines the projection bordering the dome of the foot, which is divided by four cartouches linked by festoons of laurel leaves; each cartouche encloses a symbol of the Eucharist. The knop is urn-shaped; festoons adorn its middle portion, while matte acanthus leaves support the bottom and an interlaced frieze encircles the upper edge. The two collars knops above and below the knop itself are each decorated with a frieze of Vitruvian scrolls. The gilt-lined, bell-shaped cup is held in a calyx decorated with openwork; lanceolate leaves adorn its bottom section. On four medallions surmounted by ribbons, Eucharistic symbols alternate with sheaves of wheat, bunches of grapes, and vine leaves. The resultant composition is a convincing example of Louis XVI Neo-Classicism.

A large *Censer* (NGC 14815) produced by Amiot twenty-five years later in 1837 displays the same aesthetic. An excellent designer, Amiot creates a clear, well-balanced composition in the form of a Classical urn decorated with gadroons, interlacing, and a lance-and-dart motif. As usual, these carefully chosen motifs do justice to the surfaces they cover and enhance the unity of the work.

The importation into Quebec of censers and chalices made in Paris at the workshop of Jean-Charles Cahier (1772–c. 1849) between 1819 and 1838, which are essentially variations on the same themes, helped spread Amiot's aesthetic. The three works examined above are merely examples of what is, without doubt, the single most important body of work produced by a Quebec silversmith in the five decades between about 1790 and 1840, in terms of both quality and quantity. Indeed, his style spread so rapidly throughout the Quebec City region that Ranvoyzé began to imitate it as early as 1788. After 1800, it gradually permeated the entire Montreal region. Amiot was thus responsible for initiating a profound change in the nature of the liturgical silver produced in Lower Canada.

Although best known for bringing the Louis XVI style to Quebec, Amiot was also drawn to British Neo-Classicism, evident especially in the articles he produced for domestic use. A small set comprising a *Milk Jug, Sugar Bowl, and Sugar Tongs with the Arms of the Chaussegros de Léry Family* (NGC 24097.1–3) was made during the same period as the *Ewer* (fig. 4) described earlier, but represents a different trend. The oval sugar bowl, matching milk jug, and delicate sugar tongs with elegant arms are all consistent with the late Adam style and are among the few manifestations of this aesthetic in the artist's body of work. Just a short time later, in response to changing tastes, he began to favour the Regency style, which prized grandeur above all other qualities, to the detriment of aesthetic justifications for the manner in which decorative elements were combined. His style of ornamentation became more sculptural. Despite their small dimensions, early pieces such as the *Wine Funnel* (NGC 24070), the *Pap-boat* (NGC 25058), and the *Christening Mug of Helen Scott Black* (NGC 24141) already exhibit the full forms characteristic of this trend. Interestingly, Amiot referred to the pap-boat's shape (a pap-boat literally looks like a boat, occasionally with flat handles) as inspiration in numerous baptismal ewers, demonstrating the impact of domestic silver on the formal evolution of liturgical silver. Shaped like a Greek krater vase and decorated with austere gadrooning, the presentation *Cup* (fig. 34) he made several years later is an even better example of the highly sculptural Regency style, although in this case the ornamentation is well suited to the shapes it embellishes.[43] A distinctive *Sauce Tureen* (see fig. 5) also from around 1825 is based on contemporary porcelain work. In the finest Classical tradition, the finish is flawless, rivalling the workmanship of the best English and French silversmiths of the period.

Amiot's references to both forms of European Neo-Classicism – French and English – were in themselves quite unusual, but he also created original syntheses of the two movements. A *Ciborium* (NGC 24778) in this collection is an example of

Fig. 35
Laurent Amiot
Quebec City 1764–1839
Coffee Pot from the Le Moine Family c. 1796
Silver and mahogany
NGC, Gift of Suzy M. Simard, Westmount, Quebec 1994, in memory of Dr and Mme Guy Hamel (37674)

Fig. 36
Laurent Amiot
Quebec City 1764–1839
Soup Tureen with the Monogram of the Hertel de Rouville Family c. 1790
Silver
Private collection

one such work. The design, proportions, and use of large bare surfaces and the natural lustre of the silver give the vessel an austerity consistent with the Louis XVI aesthetic. However, the calyx, entirely formed of embossed gadrooning, appears to have been borrowed from an early-nineteenth-century English cup or ewer. This hybrid mode was clearly successful, since the silversmith frequently repeated the formula.

Along with the two Neo-Classical styles, Amiot often incorporated elements of the Rococo into his work. The most obvious example is perhaps the distinctive *Coffee Pot from the Le Moine Family* (fig. 35), the only known silver coffee pot produced in pre-industrial Quebec. The body of the vessel is shaped very much like a Classical urn, and its ornamentation is in keeping with this choice. Moulding, beading, foliated garlands, and interlacing combine in a way that enhances the French character suggested by the object's shape. However, the mahogany handle and heavy acanthus leaves on the swan-neck spout appear to echo the English Rococo style. The handle was probably sculpted by François Baillairgé, who may also have provided models for the spout, the handle sockets, and the knob on the lid, all of which were cast.[44] Nor was this an isolated project on Amiot's part, but rather an example of an ongoing effort to combine styles. During this same period Amiot adopted a similar approach in designing his *Soup Tureen with the Arms of the Hertel de Rouville Family* (fig. 36). The convex, elongated body and spherical, clawed feet recall the English Rococo period, while the shape of the lid and the ornamentation, including the generous festoons of embossed laurels encircling the paunch, are derived from the Louis XVI style.[45]

Victorian Neo-Classicism

Starting in the 1830s, silversmithing, like other artistic disciplines, began to reflect various historical styles almost simultaneously in a movement known as historicism. Victorian Neo-Classicism was the first of these trends. The original Neo-Classical tradition did not suddenly disappear in 1830, the date generally mentioned as marking its demise, but continued until about 1860: the Victorians reinterpreted Neo-Classicism in various ways, making it their own. For example, rules of proportion were no longer so strictly applied. This new Classical revival seemed more faithful to the letter than the spirit of the style.

François Sasseville (1797–1864) and Pierre Lespérance (1819–1882), both trained by Laurent Amiot, were his direct and true artistic heirs. Each was a sensitive and intelligent artist, and each enriched his legacy from the master by making it relevant to his own era. Sasseville, who produced numerous place settings and utensils for the Nairne family, created a striking *Teapot* (fig. 37) around 1840, which displays the monogram of John Nairne, the seigneur of Murray Bay.[46] Whether we consider its cylindrical oval shape, the straight spout emerging from the base, or the delicately engraved motifs on the friezes at top and bottom, clearly the artist borrowed directly from the late Adam style, fashionable half a century earlier. At other times he varied his other approaches, for example, in an *Aspersorium* (see fig. 38) which imitates a Greek krater. If its proportions were less massive, and if certain details such as the handle and cherub-head attachments as well as the heavy gadrooning and lance-and-dart motifs were not present, we would be tempted to credit Sasseville with reviving a style that was popular in about 1825. Finally, the *Chalice* (see fig. 10) in silver and gold that he made around 1850 is the product of an unusual synthesis. The historiated cartouches on the foot and the gadrooned knop recall the Louis XVI style and act as a reminder of his apprenticeship to Amiot. Despite these French touches, the cup itself reinterprets an English Regency design dating from about 1820, as much by its form as by its decoration.[47] For example, we recognize the characteristic thistle inside the cup and the gadrooned calyx encasing the lower portion and surmounted by a wide foliated frieze and bunches of grapes that climb halfway up the sides. The vine leaves and grapes are a motif that can be found on secular drinking cups of the

Fig. 37
François Sasseville
Sainte-Anne-de-la-Pocatière, Quebec 1797 – Quebec City 1864
Teapot with the Monogram of the Nairne Family c. 1840
Silver and mahogany
NGC, purchased 1974 (18074.1)

Regency period, but here they appear in their guise of traditional symbols of the Eucharist. Note the impeccable workmanship, especially on the dynamic frieze that encircles the calyx. Such a dramatic combination of pure English Regency and French Neo-Classical, as opposed to Amiot's more blended approach, would have been inconceivable a generation before. It was, however, totally in line with the tenets of Victorian Neo-Classicism.

Pierre Lespérance worked with Sasseville for several years and inherited many of his clients when he died, prolonging the Classical revival well into the nineteenth century. Among many works that demonstrate this, one of the most telling examples is Lespérance's *Pair of Sauce-boats* (NGC 27852.1–2) from Cyrille Tessier's collection. At first glance, they appear to recall the beginning of the nineteenth century. A second look at their size and proportions, heavy handles and feet, and unusually thick metal makes it obvious they were created much later in the century, between 1840 and 1880. A similar examination of the *Butter Dish* (NGC 24931) he made around the same time leads to the same conclusion.

Fig. 38
François Sasseville
Sainte-Anne-de-la-Pocatière, Quebec 1797 – Quebec City 1864
Aspersorium and Aspergillum c. 1840–60
Silver
NGC, Gift of the Henry Birks Collection of Canadian Silver, 1979 (27740.1–2)

Several other silversmiths who were active during this period responded to its particular demands by specializing in the production of tableware and small accessories. Like other categories of silver, flatware underwent a stylistic change. The fiddle pattern, introduced around 1820, became almost traditional within a remarkably short time. After 1840, utensils increased dramatically in size and began to be made from heavy, thick metal. Changing table manners also led to the creation of new types of utensils, such as the Stilton scoop, which appeared in about 1840; one of the first known examples of a *Stilton Scoop* (NGC 37716) was produced by Peter Bohle.

Neo-Rococo

During the period when Victorian Neo-Classicism was flourishing, there was a concurrent return to mid-eighteenth century forms. The Neo-Rococo movement was characterized by supple, sinuous lines and a decorative vocabulary highlighting the volute. In the mid-1800s, it was the single most popular international style among manufacturers.

Dating from about 1850, the *Ewer* (see fig. 17) by David Bohle was among the first manifestations of this style in Quebec. It is immediately obvious that the vessel is derived from a basic design used in about 1780, during the transitional period between Rococo and Neo-Classicism. However, Bohle employed the design only as the starting point for a free and innovative rendering. He began by vertically compressing the work, an idea he may have borrowed from a turn-of-the-century milk jug, and which set the tone for the whole. While most contemporary ewers were essentially circular, this one is based on an elongated oval: the paunch, in the shape of an inverted pear, is flattened and supports a disproportionately long and rigid neck. The long, broad spout at the end of the neck does not appear to be particularly functional. What is more, its shape and lack of fluidity clash with the form of the handle, which, although similar in style to handles produced in the 1780s, is on an extreme slant. The conflict produces a certain incoherence in the overall design, an incoherence echoed by the foot and knop: the foot is Classically simple, with plain moulding, and flattened in a way that makes the knop stand alone rather than blending it into the base. This leaves room for a certain amount of ornamentation on the knop, which is the only section adorned with engraved chased roses, a Rococo motif confirming the silversmith's stylistic allegiances. All these aspects taken together, along with the sacrifice of functionality to decoration, demonstrate the eclectic sensibility prevailing at the time.

Robert Hendery (1814–1897) is the name most often associated with Neo-Rococo silver in Quebec. His workshop, the most important of the second half of the nineteenth century, produced a multiplicity of works in this style. Among them is a *Christening Mug* (NGC 25208) made around 1860. Globular in form, its ornamentation consists of large C-shaped volutes in a rocaille fragment, combined

Fig. 39
Robert Hendery
Corfu 1814 – Montreal 1897
Speaking-trumpet Presented to
William Perry 1860
Silver, with yellow and black silk braids
NGC, purchased 1993 (37137)

Fig. 40
Robert Hendery (for Savage, Lyman and Co.)
Corfu 1814 – Montreal 1897
Teapot c. 1868–78
Silver
NGC, Gift of the Henry Birks Collection of Canadian Silver, 1979 (27916)

with bouquets of roses in bloom. Shaped like a large question mark, the handle is harmoniously integrated into the composition. No similar harmony between form and ornamentation is evident in the *Speaking-trumpet Presented to William Perry* (fig. 39), which Hendery created the same year. Rather, there is a marked contrast between the pure, functional form of the speaking-trumpet and the typically Neo-Rococo motifs of the decoration, especially the cartouche highlighting the inscription and the bouquets of roses around the bell. The work illustrates just how profoundly the Neo-Rococo style had taken root. By 1860, the very notion of ornamentation had come to be symbolized by elements of its decorative vocabulary, which had achieved the status of archetypes. Based solely on the number of pieces produced, Neo-Rococo was indisputably the dominant style of the mid-nineteenth century, and its expressions could be found in every household.

It was not always employed in such a hackneyed way. For example, the design of the *Teapot* (fig. 40) produced by Hendery for Savage, Lyman and Company a few years later displays much more coherence. Shaped like an inverted pear and resting on a small base decorated with moulding, it is considerably more squat than its Rococo precursors. The body is ornamented with enormous cartouches and rosebuds, which also adorn the lid. Most of the motifs are rendered without great finesse, as if they were intended to do no more than cover the surface. The handle, which describes a perfect, large *C*, is free of decoration, as is the matching spout. Their austerity sets them apart from the body, while linking them visually to the moulded foot.

Neo-Baroque

In the mid-nineteenth century, revivals of historical styles occurred with such regularity that often the new styles and the earlier ones coexisted side by side. This produced a stylistic mélange reflected in a large number of works. It is in this context that the Neo-Baroque movement emerged towards 1850. Although many commissions for the Catholic Church were done in the Victorian Neo-Classical style, following secular practice, the church sought a means to assert a separate presence and identity. As a result, the Neo-Baroque style is seen most frequently in liturgical pieces. The movement often made use of forms that were in fashion from about 1660 to 1720, but its pursuit of splendour occasionally resulted in the creation of bold syntheses. Lavish historiated motifs frequently ornament holy vessels produced in this style.

A *Monstrance* (NGC 16869) created by François Sasseville in 1852 reflects the new trend. The heavy, over-elaborate base attests to the distant influence of Neo-Classicism, and contrasts with the clean lines of the unadorned sun, which is reminiscent of works produced during the 1660s. These two elements combine with an eclectic mixture of decorative motifs to produce a work that is distinctly Neo-Baroque. A *Ciborium* (fig. 41) by the same silversmith reflects the same aesthetic, although it features different motifs. Here, the lanceolate leaves, fluting, and gadrooning are reminiscent of the Grand Siècle style of seventeenth-century silver, while the calyx is embellished with historiated motifs: medallions portraying Christ, the Virgin Mary, and Saint John, evoking the Passion, and sheaves of wheat, bunches of grapes, and bulrushes, symbolizing the Eucharist.

Created some thirty-five years after Sasseville's *Monstrance*, a *Chalice* (NGC 24607) made by Ambroise Lafrance (1847–1905) around 1885 demonstrates, by its very existence, that the enthusiasm for the Neo-Baroque style endured for quite some time. The calyx as well as the dome of the foot has a generous selection of historiated motifs. The medallions on the cup represent the three Virtues – Faith, Hope, and Charity – while those on the dome depict the Adoration of the Magi, the Flight into Egypt, and the Crucifixion. As the century progressed, historiated ornamentation became excessively anecdotal. However, this chalice can still be classified as Neo-Baroque due to its massive proportions, which show how the style tended to magnify the dimensions of works, giving them a rather emphatic, even

Fig. 41

François Sasseville

Sainte-Anne-de-la-Pocatière, Quebec 1797 – Quebec City 1864

Ciborium c. 1860

Silver and gold

NGC, Gift of the Henry Birks Collection of Canadian Silver, 1979 (24800)

somewhat bombastic, charm. Fundamentally ostentatious, this revival exhibits little of the harmony and vivacity characteristic of the authentic Baroque movement.

Naturalism

One of the most prevalent sentiments of the nineteenth century, the love of nature was esteemed by Neo-Classicists and exalted by Romanticists. The Naturalist movement is testimony to this interest. Placing a distinct emphasis on fauna and flora, Naturalism had a multifaceted impact on ornamentation. The style reached its zenith in Quebec silver during the 1850s and 1860s. In this period, in which the lines between art and ornamentation blurred, the Naturalist style exercised a profound influence on contemporary taste, even dictating the themes of ornaments. Moreover, the moral connotations associated with the study of nature were just as attractive to artists as to the public. Naturalism drew its inspiration from the publications of J.C. Loudon, especially *Gardener's Magazine* (1826–1843), and from the horticultural projects of his wife, Jane. Sir Joseph Paxton, the Duke of Devonshire's head gardener, who led a life entirely devoted to nature, personified this movement in the public eye. In North America, the trend was reflected in the publications of A.J. Downing.

The *Salver* (fig. 42) – a tray with feet used for carrying small objects – presented to Duncan McFarland is a rarity within the context of Quebec silver.[48] Particularly interesting for its originality of form and ornamentation, this salver is designed to resemble a painting. The border, resembling a heavy picture frame, is composed of cast and applied sections, which highlight the smooth floor of the tray. This is rendered more delicately; on it, we find the inscription, encircled by finely engraved volutes. The artist responds to the influence of his era by borrowing elements of various styles: eclecticism is particularly evident in the combination of the somewhat rigid, curved outline, evidence of the Rococo revival, with the palmettes on the pitted surface of the feet, a Regency touch. The floor of the salver displays a wide frieze of foliage with freely rendered volutes, providing additional Rococo accents. However, the border is interspersed with vine leaves pointing towards the centre, a motif which is Naturalistic in feel. Testimony to a period that has yet to reveal all its secrets, this salver is one of the first manifestations of the Naturalist style in Canadian silver.

Interestingly, Robert Hendery also played a key role in the diffusion of Naturalism. The ornamentation of the *Hunt Cup of the Montreal Fox Hounds* (NGC 24010) that he made for J.R. Harper and Company in 1882 consists of references to the club's various activities. Formal coherence is completely abandoned in favour of allegorical design. The circular base beneath the three riding whips which support the cup is scarcely decorated: a single motif of foliage adorns the foot. On the cup itself, which is shaped like a flattened cone, a vine wreath encircles the inscription, while horseshoes on either side serve as handles.

Fig. 42
Peter Bohle
Montreal 1786–1862
Salver Presented to Duncan McFarland c. 1840–50
Silver
NGC, purchased 1996 (38262)

In its most extreme manifestations, Naturalism led to the creation of bizarre-looking objects such as the receptacle Henry Birks and Sons made for the Connecticut Valley Poultry Association in Vermont. Awarded annually to the owner of the best rooster in the region, it was identified as a *Punch Bowl* (fig. 43) at the time of its acquisition by the National Gallery. If it did serve a genuine function, as the gilt interior suggests (gilt prevented chemical reactions), it is more likely to have been used as an eggnog bowl. However, it may have been strictly a competition cup – the term used by the daughter of the last treasurer of the association.[49] Be that as it may, this item is clearly the product of a most eclectic

Fig. 43
Henry Birks and Sons
Active Montreal from 1893
Punch Bowl c. 1910–15
Silver and gold
NGC, Gift of the Henry Birks Collection of Canadian Silver, 1979 (24121)

brand of Naturalism. The work borrows elements of designs developed by the Gorham company in the United States around the year 1870.[50] Resting on four chicken legs with fully extended claws, the bowl is shaped like an egg, or perhaps two chicken breasts; two roosters, facing outward, serve as handles. The front of the bowl features an engraving of the inside of a henhouse. The back, undoubtedly meant for an inscription, was left bare. These poultry motifs are very much at odds with the Classical elements that complete the ornamentation: although it is remotely possible that the overlapping motifs and acanthus leaves were intended to suggest plumage, no such explanation justifies the inclusion of purely fantastical elements such as the rosettes, the Rococo arabesques, the gadrooning, and the laurel border, not to mention the diminutive Montreal coat of arms! Lastly, the coldness of the design and the grey shade of silver make it clear that the industrial era has begun.

Canadian Naturalism

In the wake of the Naturalist trend there followed a unique and recognizable movement, Canadian Naturalism, which flourished throughout the second half of the nineteenth century. It was a political environment in which efforts were being made to define the country – Confederation would be declared on 1 July 1867 – and silversmiths also sought to create a truly national style. Thus they made frequent references to local flora and fauna, as well as to the pastimes, daily routines, and other activities of Victorian Canada. These images would rapidly turn into stereotypes. The maple leaf and beaver, in particular, became marks of identity.

Already, since about 1700 if not earlier, the maple leaf had been regarded as an appropriate national symbol. During the celebrated visit by the Prince of Wales in 1860, the maple leaf was widely used for decoration and the members of the welcoming committee displayed it as the symbol of their native land. A few years later, Alexander Muir (1830–1906), a teacher who became a school administrator, wrote *The Maple Leaf Forever*, a song celebrating Confederation, which became so popular among English Canadians that it often served as a national anthem.[51] The following year, 1868, Queen Victoria granted coats of arms featuring maple leaves to both Ontario and Quebec. When the current Canadian flag was introduced on 15 February 1965, the maple leaf was finally adopted as an official national symbol.

The beaver has an even longer history as a national symbol because it was the tribal emblem of the Hurons, who used it as a totemic signature on their treaties with the first European settlers. It was first employed as a heraldic symbol on the coat of arms bestowed upon Sir William Alexander by Charles I in 1633. In 1673, the Comte de Frontenac, the governor of New France, proposed a coat of arms for Quebec City that included "un castor de sable au chef d'or" (a black beaver on a gold ground, or, in heraldic language, a beaver passant sable on a chief or). In about 1678, the Hudson's Bay Company adopted a coat of arms featuring four of these animals. The symbol was also included in the original coat of arms of Montreal, adopted in 1833 when the city became an established municipality. In fact, the beaver was considered to be so important at the time of the fur trade that its pelt became a standard unit of exchange. The Hudson's Bay Company even issued a coin whose face value was one pelt. When Canada printed its first postage stamp on 23 April 1851, this was the image chosen. However, the beaver was not officially recognized as a national symbol until Parliament enacted legislation to this effect on 23 March 1975.[52]

The *Tea and Coffee Set Presented to John Leeming* (NGC 24122.1–4) was created during the same period as the first Canadian stamp. Designed by James Duncan (1806–1881), it was produced by the Bohle and Hendery company and engraved by George Matthews (c. 1816–1864). The set was presented to Leeming on 30 July 1851, in recognition of his efforts as Secretary-General of the Provincial Industrial Exhibition held in Montreal from 17 to 19 October of the previous year.[53] All the

Fig. 44
(detail)

pieces in the set are bulbous in form and have high bases. The squirrel finials on the *Coffee Pot* and *Teapot* (fig. 44) are a reference to local wildlife. The rest of the ornamentation is also Naturalistic: the rise of the foot of each vessel is embossed with wide oak leaves that alternate with acorns. The paunches are enveloped in boughs of maple, and a frieze of leaves encircles each top. The matte treatment given to these plant motifs and their three-dimensionality makes them stand out against the highly polished, mirror-like surfaces.

In 1859, a group of employees of the Grand Trunk Railway presented a set produced by Robert Hendery consisting of a large *Ewer, Goblets, and Tray* (NGC 26097.1–8), the latter resting on four feet, to David Stark on his retirement. Although the maple leaf frieze covering the heavy moulding on the foot of the pot-bellied ewer is a relatively common ornament, the railway scenes on the body and on the six matching cups are more unusual. On one side of the ewer is a depiction of the iron bridge spanning the Chaudière River near Lévis: the river and rapids are clearly visible.[54] The other side features the bridge that crosses the Richelieu River at Belœil. This ensemble was one of the first Canadian sets to depict local landscapes, a practice already firmly entrenched in Great Britain and the United States.

Barely two years later, in 1861, Hendery created a different kind of *Ewer* (fig. 45) for presentation to the Montreal businessman John Boston by his sisters Eleanor, Julia, Esther, and Elizabeth Phillips, under circumstances that have yet to be determined. Although the basic shape of the ewer is reminiscent of a mid-eighteenth-century English beer jug, the ornamentation is Naturalistic. The

Fig. 44
Bohle and Hendery (for Savage and Lyman)
Active Montreal c. 1850–59
After drawings by James Duncan Coleraine, Ireland 1806 – Montreal 1881
Teapot from the Tea and Coffee Set Presented to John Leeming 1851
Silver and ivory
NGC, Gift of the Henry Birks Collection of Canadian Silver, 1979 (24122.1)

Fig. 45
Robert Hendery (for Savage and Lyman)
Corfu 1814 – Montreal 1897
Ewer 1861
Silver
NGC, Gift of the Henry Birks Collection of Canadian Silver, 1979 (25139)

Fig. 45
(detail)

handle is shaped like a curved branch, which wraps around the neck and paunch with a motif of raised maple leaves. Canada is further represented by the beaver that sits on the lid. Perhaps the most typically Canadian ornaments are two scenes on the paunch, on either side of the inscription naming the recipient and donors. Naturalist compositions often include rustic scenes such as the one on the left, showing Beaver Hall, the country property of the merchant Joseph Frobisher (fig. 45, detail). The one on the right is more remarkable because it is an urban landscape: this Montreal scene depicts the intersection of Lagauchetière and Beaver Hall Hill with the Church of the Messiah on the right and the Presbyterian church of St Andrew's on the left (see fig. 45).

While the ewer was among the preferred items used by Quebec silversmiths to demonstrate their skills during the second half of the nineteenth century, a simultaneous proliferation of sporting events of all kinds led to a dramatic increase in the demand for cups and trophies, and the resultant works also attest to the influence of Canadian Naturalism. Created in about 1862, the *Field Officer's Cup for the Grand Rifle Match of the United Canada* (NGC 24005) is an early example. Here, Peter Bohle adopts an approach fairly similar to the one used by Hendery for the ewer described above. The Naturalist handle is also shaped like a branch, albeit a vine shoot rather than the limb of a maple tree. It too clings to the body of the tankard, sending out leaves and scroll-shaped shoots that reach across the vessel; the motifs are repeated in the base moulding. Note that this style of ornamentation was not uniquely Canadian: it occupied a place of honour during the Regency period. Local flavour is imparted to the composition by the small, cast, beaver finial on the lid – a somewhat timid affirmation of a national identity that merely hints at the much clearer and more assertive manifestations to come.

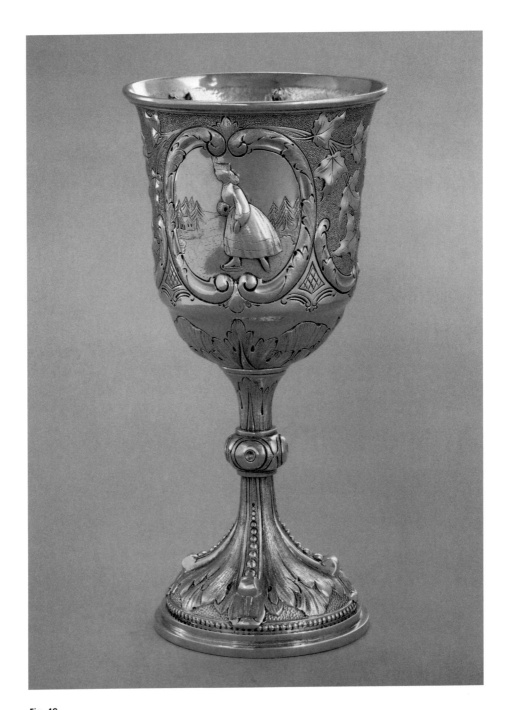

Fig. 46
Robert Hendery (for Gustavus Seifert)
Corfu 1814 – Montreal 1897
Quebec Skating Club Cup c. 1864
Silver
NGC, Gift of the Henry Birks Collection of Canadian Silver, 1979 (25140)

Fig. 47
P. Poulin
Quebec, nineteenth century
*Commemorative Trowel, Quebec City Post
Office* 1871
Silver
NGC, Gift of the Henry Birks Collection of
Canadian Silver, 1979 (25137)

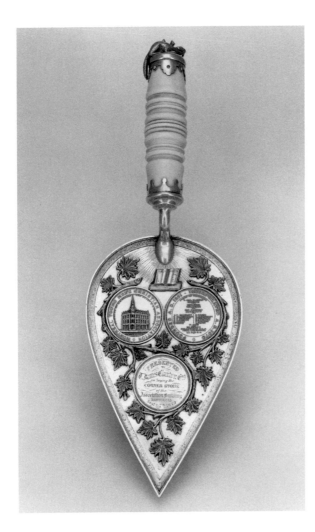

Fig. 48
Robert Hendery
Corfu 1814 – Montreal 1897
After drawings by Alfred Sandham
Montreal 1838 – Toronto 1910
*Commemorative Trowel, Montreal
YMCA* 1872
Silver, gold, and ivory
Private collection

Several historiated trophies refer to specific aspects of the daily life of the time, including popular sporting activities such as shooting, riding, snowshoeing, skating, and curling. For example, the sides of the *Quebec Skating Club Cup* (fig. 46), also made by Hendery, display two large Neo-Rococo cartouches, one of which is reserved for the obligatory inscription, while the other encloses a female figure skating on ice, with fir trees in the background. The space between the two cartouches is completely occupied by branches of maple leaves in relief against a matte ground.

In a contemporary piece, the *Gallwey Tankard of the Stadacona Curling Club of Quebec City* (NGC 25146) made about 1864, Hendery has produced a traditional covered tankard. The wreath of thistles around the inscription is hardly surprising – it was the Scots who introduced the sport of curling to Canada. The cover is crowned by the figure of a curler, serving as the knob, while two brooms decorate the base of the handle, leaving no doubt about the sport celebrated by the trophy.

Fig. 49
Robert Hendery (for Savage, Lyman and Co.)
Corfu 1814 – Montreal 1897
Inkstand c. 1869 (image rotated 180°)
Silver
NGC, Gift of the Henry Birks Collection of Canadian Silver, 1979 (25309)

As an extra flourish, the silversmith has added a large embossed beaver walking on maple leaves directly beneath the wreath of thistles. Designs like this helped integrate foreign symbols such as the thistle into the local culture.

The *Alexandra Snow Shoe Club Cup* (NGC 25237) made by Robert Hendery and Company around 1872 presents a different concept: the shaft on which such cups usually rest is replaced here by three intertwined snowshoes attached to a base. Many different versions of this design were produced, depending on the nature of the award: the riding whips supporting the *Hunt Cup* (NGC 24010) described above are an example.

Nationalism stamped its mark on other types of silver as well. Children's cups produced in the second half of the nineteenth century borrowed elements from several genres, some Naturalistic in style. A particularly eloquent example is Hendery's *Christening Mug of Edmund Stimson Wright* (NGC 25205), created sometime between 1868 and 1878. The simple cylindrical shape is set off by a massive

Fig. 50
Robert Hendery (for Savage and Lyman)
Corfu 1814 – Montreal 1897
Inkstand c. 1859–67
Silver and crystal
NGC, Gift of the Henry Birks Collection of Canadian Silver, 1979 (25288.1–3)

handle, and the gleaming surface serves as the background for a large engraving of a beaver seated on maple leaves.

The *Commemorative Trowel* (fig. 47) made by P. Poulin (nineteenth century) to mark the laying of the first stone for the Quebec City post office at a ceremony held 17 July 1871 also features a beaver, employing the motif in an original way – as the handle. The animal is shown crouched on a tree trunk, which it is gnawing, and its tail and the trunk together grasp the blade of the trowel. The large seal of Canada engraved above the inscription on the blade is surrounded by a maple wreath. This choice of iconography is particularly apt as the piece was intended to commemorate the construction of a government building.

Created a year later by Robert Hendery, the *Commemorative Trowel* (fig. 48) made for the laying of the cornerstone for the YMCA in Montreal is designed quite differently. Three medallions decorate the blade and a piece of turned ivory forms the handle, introducing a third colour to the silver and gold of the metals. National references appear in the maple branches between the medallions and the small beaver on the handle, emphasizing the importance of these symbols.

The former is particularly prominent in an *Inkstand* (fig. 49) by Hendery made about 1869, which is actually in the form of a naturalistically rendered maple leaf. The stem is coiled into a pen holder, while rosebuds entwined around the circular opening designed to hold a glass ink vial represent England.

Another, slightly earlier *Inkstand* (fig. 50) by the same maker features other aspects of the Canadian landscape. The top of the stand evokes a desolate northern landscape; a caribou stands between the two inkwells. Several fallen branches litter the stony ground, while a dead tree trunk on the left spreads dry roots over the thin soil, lending credibility to the scene. Several copies were made of this item.[55]

The Modernist Influence of Art Deco

The first half of the twentieth century was marked by the gradual expansion of Henry Birks and Sons until, ultimately, it monopolized the Canadian silver trade. First consolidating its position in Quebec, the company promptly outstripped its competitors in the rest of the country. By the 1940s, the Birks empire stretched all the way from Halifax to Victoria.[56] Since most of the silver articles turned out during these years were industrially produced and intended for the mass market, their designs are generally conservative and repetitive. It was not until after the Second World War that a modest amount of experimentation occurred. The Functionalist movement, which had originated in the early twentieth century in Europe, emerged during this period as a commanding presence in architecture as well as in the decorative arts. Whatever their leanings, creators from all fields were profoundly affected by this vision, according to which form, to be considered beautiful, must adapt to function. In silver, this influence can be noted in work produced in the late 1930s, the 1940s, and especially the early 1950s, visible in the forms of the pieces. In an interesting parallel trend, Functionalist artists also introduced the widespread use of such precious materials as ivory and ebony.

The Montreal silversmith Gilles Beaugrand (b. 1906) was among the first to assimilate these influences. Having trained in Paris in the workshops of Edgar Brant, Szabo, and Richard Desvallières, Beaugrand produced both liturgical pieces and hollow ware. Unfortunately, none of his work has yet been added to the National Gallery's collection.[57]

Georges Delrue (b. 1920), though known primarily as a jeweller, was also a silversmith early in his career.[58] His works attest to the influence of the Modernist Art Deco movement, which became very popular in North America during the 1930s. His *Pair of Candlesticks* (NGC 28636.1–2) from 1950–51 makes use of the noble materials silver and ebony in a rigorous design that incorporates simple geometric shapes, right angles, and a series of circles. His trapezoidal *Salt and Pepper Shakers* (fig. 51) from a couple of years later feature distinctive, stylized letters outlined in subtle relief on the front of each shaker.

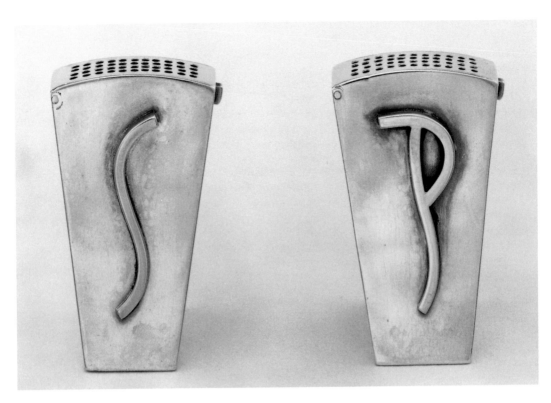

Fig. 51
Georges Delrue
Tourcoing, France 1920
Salt and Pepper Shakers c. 1953–55
Silver and gold
NGC, purchased 1984 (28637.1–2)

There was a sharp decline in the production of silver in Quebec and the rest of Canada after the fifties, although artists such as Beaugrand, Delrue, and Raymond Bégin (b. 1923) continued to accept commissions, especially from the Roman Catholic Church. However, the Functionalist concept came to dominate the art world to the point that form, and not the use of precious materials, was now the priority. As a result, silver was soon supplanted by other materials.

In the course of a long history, silverwork in Quebec has been affected by a variety of formal tendencies, from Mannerism to Art Deco, witness to the constant influence of the major European trends. The unique context presented by New France and Quebec has led to the introduction of a note of true originality into this production.

Notes

1. Dufrenne 1968.

2. Schapiro 1994, p. 51.

3. The Royal Ontario Museum owns a *Plate* by Paradis, bearing the same coats of arms (950.215). The work is reproduced in Trudel 1974b, p. 219.

4. He was one of the first Quebec silversmiths to be the subject of a fairly substantial monograph. See Morisset 1945c.

5. The two candlesticks previously belonged to the collector Louis Carrier, who probably acquired them from the council of churchwardens. The candlestick by Paul Lambert was purchased by Henry Birks on 10 January 1949, and donated to the National Gallery, with the rest of the collection, in 1979. The Parisian candlestick (A.60.263.0), which remained in the Carrier collection, was acquired by the Musée de la province de Québec, now the Musée du Québec, in 1959.

6. This notion has barely been examined to date. However, the exhibition catalogue from the Musée du Québec (*François Ranvoyzé* 1968), for example, which concentrates on liturgical silver, clearly demonstrates the importance of the Baroque style. The collections of the churches at Saint-Augustin-de-Desmaures and the church at L'Islet-sur-Mer contain many of his works of this type, indicating that he maintained close ties with Louis-Michel Bériau and Jacques Panet, the priests of these parishes. The works they commissioned were often almost archaic even at the time, demonstrating that a faction of the Roman Catholic Church remained attached to the art of the Ancien Régime.

7. Concerning François Ranvoyzé's training, see Derome 1976.

8. Apart from the *Ewer of François Ranvoyzé*, the domestic ewers include the *Ewer Belonging to Abbé Louis-Michel Bériau* (NGC 27774), owned by the National Gallery, and another which is housed at the Collège Sainte-Anne-de-la-Pocatière in La Pocatière, Quebec. The baptismal ewer commissioned by the Saint-Michel-de-Yamaska council of churchwardens in 1783 is presently owned by the Musée du Québec (A.69.268.0). Jean Trudel points out the existence of a reproduction in Trudel 1984, p. 252. Finally, the *Baptismal Ewer* (NGC 24601) made for the Sault-au-Récollet parish in 1788 is now in the National Gallery's collection. An examination of the altar cruet sets made by Ranvoyzé, in which the pieces are actually miniature ewers, again points to older Parisian models.

9. The earliest dated object on which this new style was observed is the ciborium commissioned by the Saint-Roch-des-Aulnaies parish in 1782. The work is currently deposited at the Montreal Museum of Fine Arts (218-1996).

10. The Musée du Québec owns three works displaying such friezes: a tea caddy by Charles Aldridge (78.407), a coffee pot by Robert and David Hennel (78.406), and a tea urn by John Schofield (78.405).

11. The presentation on 4 October 1750 was probably a mere formality, and it is unlikely that the monstrance had arrived yet. In fact, its charge and discharge marks were not registered in Paris until 1 October 1750, just three days earlier. The cross finial was added later.

12. Hare 1987, p. 324.

13. Ibid., p. 322.

14. Noppen 1991.

15. Noppen 1990.

16. Alcouffe 1986.

17. Villeneuve 1997, pp. 110, 111.

18. The first date probably indicates when they were made, while the second is that of the client's death.

19. ANQQ. Register of the notary J.B. Planté, no. 2508, 8 Nov. 1800.

20. Traditionally, the metals used by silversmiths were silver and gold, but in 1742 Thomas Boulsover discovered a cheaper method, which became known as Sheffield plate after the home town of the inventor. The procedure consisted of using heat to lay a fine skin of silver over both sides of a sheet of copper – explaining why pieces in Sheffield silver present smooth surfaces without engraving. A disadvantage is that repeated polishing tends to remove the thin layer of silver, exposing the copper base. Although Quebec silversmiths did not use this technique, the existence of such pieces affected their treatment of forms.

21. Among the pieces acquired by Leslie are also a pair of goblets, a pair of wine-bottle coasters, a pair of salt dishes and matching mustard pot, a serving spoon, a marrow scoop, a fish slice, a wine funnel, a snuffer, asparagus tongs, and place settings for a dozen guests, all in solid silver and bearing the family coat of arms. The Montreal silversmith George Savage was later commissioned to create another pair of salt dishes to complete the set. Matching utensils were purchased from other Montreal makers. A coffee pot (NGC 24017.4) made by Robert Hendery for Savage and Lyman completed the tea set in the second half of the nineteenth century. In the same period as the London silver, Leslie also acquired other domestic articles, these ones in Sheffield plate: a covered sauce tureen, a coffee pot, a pair of wine coolers, and a muffin tray, all likewise inscribed with the family arms. A pair of round plate warmers without the coat of arms may have also been purchased at this time. Given the cost, it was customary for a large household to acquire such items in Sheffield plate rather than solid silver. Aside from the tea set and matching coffee pot, housed today at the National Gallery of Canada, all these pieces are owned by Leslie's descendants.

22. Grimwade 1985.

23. For more on John Neilson, see Le Jeune 1931.

24. Normand 1983.

25. Villeneuve 1987.

26. For more on Cruickshank, see Derome 1983b.

27. ANQM. Register of the notary Antoine Foucher, no. 4735, 17 Sept. 1781.

28. ANQM. Ibid., no. 4732, 15 September 1781. In the entry, the month originally entered has been replaced by "October," indicating that the contract was not signed at the time it was drawn up.

29. ANQM. Register of Jean-Baptiste Desève, no. 3, 21 Aug. 1785.

30. Villeneuve 1997, pp. 58–62.

31. Archives, council of churchwardens, Notre-Dame de Montréal, Montreal. Box 1790. Invoice of P. Huguet, 28 Dec. 1794.

32. IBC, Gérard-Morisset fonds: archives, councils of churchwardens, Saint-Jean-Baptiste, Rouville, Sainte-Rose (Île-Jésus), and Sainte-Anne-des-Plaines, in the file for Huguet, dit Latour, Pierre.

33. ANQM. Register of Jean-Baptiste Desève, no. 2117, 20 Dec. 1803.

34. ANQM. Ibid., no. 1459, 23 July 1798.

35. In 1810, he was hired by his former master and was exclusively employed for one year on making liturgical pieces. See ANQM, register of Jean-Baptiste Latour, no. 540, 14 June 1810.

36. For more on Smillie, see Allodi and Tovell 1989.

37. A commemorative cup dating from 1826, currently owned by the Royal Ontario Museum (L.982.18.1), is the earliest testimony to his activities.

38. *Montreal Herald* 1834.

39. On François Baillairgé's contribution as a sculptor, see Villeneuve 1997, pp. 62–78 and 138–75.

40. Villeneuve 1988.

41. ANQQ. Register of Antoine A.(braham) Parent, no. 255, 21 Dec. 1816.

42. ANQQ. Ibid., no. 7912, 20 June 1836.

43. This cup had at one point been used for presentation purposes. The inscription was removed at a later date.

44. François Baillairgé generally supplied Laurent Amiot with teapot handles and knobs, soup-tureen handles, and urn knobs. In the late spring of 1796, he sent the silversmith "les modèles du pot d'argent, un bec, deux douilles d'anse et le petit vase du couvercle" (the models for the silver vessel, a spout, two handle sockets, and the small knob for the cover). Amiot paid for the models three days later. On 15 December of the same year, Baillairgé sent him a coffee-pot handle. It appears that these are all components of the *Coffee Pot from the Le Moine Family*. See ANQQ, François Baillairgé fonds: "Journal de François Baillairgé," 30 May, 3 June, and 15 Dec. 1796.

45. Contrary to Quebec standard practice, the maker engraved the object's weight underneath: *9 MAR : 3 ONCS et MIE* (9 marks, 3.5 ounces; a mark is 8 ounces).

46. For more on the Nairne family and the Murray Bay seigneury, see Wrong 1926.

47. Numerous Regency goblets were based on this model. One such piece, made by Samuel Hennel, is in the collection of The Metropolitan Museum of Art in New York. See McNab 1981, p. 88. In addition, see *Fine English* 1988, no. 232.

48. Only one other salver made in Quebec is currently known, by William Farquhar (known in Montreal from 1823–42); it is now at the Winnipeg Art Gallery (G-89-96).

49. NGC curatorial files. Letter from Mrs James T. Corvan to Henry Birks and Company [*sic*], 2 Nov. 1979.

50. The ice bowl produced by the Gorham Manufacturing Company, designed in 1870 and made in 1871, is similarly constructed: the vaguely semi-spherical bowl represents a glacier, with two polar bears, serving as handles, perched on either side. Dating from approximately the same era as the work by Henry Birks and Sons is a punch bowl attributed to Joseph Heinrich. The canoe-shaped bowl has handles in the form of heads of Indian warriors. See Venable 1996, pp. 197–99.

51. Green 1994.

52. *Heraldry in Canada*. Ottawa: National Archives of Canada, 1969.

53. *Montreal Gazette* 1851; *Montreal Transcript* 1851, p. 2; *Morning Chronicle* 1851.

54. *Montreal Gazette* 1859.

55. The Henry Birks Collection of Canadian Silver includes another inkstand (NGC 25287) identical to this one. The glass vials, intact on the second example, are quite remarkable.

56. See chapter one of this publication for the complete history.

57. For more on Gilles Beaugrand, see Gauvreau 1940b, pp. 191–96, and Déziel 1951a.

58. For more on Georges Delrue, see Fournier 1947 and Déziel 1951b.

BIBLIOGRAPHY

A. PRIMARY SOURCES

I. Manuscripts

Archives, Augustine Monastery of the Hôtel-Dieu de Québec, Quebec City.

Archives, Augustine Monastery of the Hôpital-Général, Quebec City.

Archives, Canadian Guild of Crafts, Quebec (formerly the Canadian Handicrafts Guild), Montreal.

Archives, council of churchwardens, Saint-Charles-Borromée, Charlesbourg.

Archives, council of churchwardens, Notre-Dame de Montréal, Montreal.

Archives, council of churchwardens, Notre-Dame de Québec, Quebec City.

Archives, council of churchwardens, Saint-Pierre, Île-d'Orléans.

Archives of American Art, Washington Center, Washington, D.C., Francis Patrick Garvan fonds.

Archives nationales du Québec, Montreal (ANQM).

Archives nationales du Québec, Quebec City (ANQQ).

Archives, Séminaire de Québec, Quebec City.

Archives, Ursuline Monastery, Quebec City.

Canadian Museum of Civilisation, Hull (CMC, formerly National Museum of Man).

Inventaire des biens culturels du Québec, Department of Cultural Affairs, Musée du Québec, Quebec City (IBC).

Library of Goldsmiths' Hall, London, England.

National Archives of Canada, Ottawa (NAC, formerly Public Archives of Canada).

National Gallery of Canada, Ottawa (NGC).

II. Publications

Les Annales de l'Hôtel-Dieu de Québec, 1639–1716. Selections, edited and with an introduction by Dom Albert Jamet. Quebec City: Hôtel-Dieu, 1939.

Documents relatifs à la monnaie, au change et aux finances du Canada sous le régime français. Selected, edited, and with commentaries and an introduction by Adam Shortt. 2 vols. Ottawa: National Archives of Canada, 1925.

Rapport de l'archiviste de la province de Québec, 1921–22. Quebec City: Louis-Amable Proulx, 1922, pp. 237–61.

Rapport de l'archiviste de la province de Québec, 1957–58 et 1958–59. Quebec City: Rédempti Paradis, 1959, pp. 359–79.

Relations des Jésuites. 6 vols. Montreal: Éditions du Jour, 1972.

B. SECONDARY SOURCES

Books and Articles

The initials *DCB* refer to the *Dictionary of Canadian Biography* (Toronto: University of Toronto Press, 1969–).

Ahlborn 1968 – Ahlborn, Richard E. "Canadiana at the Smithsonian." *Canadian Antiques Collector* 3:5 (May 1968), pp. 7–10.

Album-souvenir **1923** – *Album-souvenir de la Basilique de Notre-Dame de Québec.* Quebec City: The Basilica, 1923.

Alcouffe 1986 – Alcouffe, Daniel. "La naissance de la table à manger au XVIIIᵉ siècle." In *La table et le partage.* Paris: La documentation française, 1986, pp. 57–65.

Allaire 1910 – Allaire, Jean-Baptiste Antoine. *Dictionnaire biographique du clergé canadien-français: Les anciens.* Montreal: Imprimerie de l'École catholique des sourds-muets, 1910.

Allodi 1974 – Allodi, Mary. *Canadian Watercolours and Drawings in the Royal Ontario Museum.* Vol. 1. Toronto: Royal Ontario Museum, 1974.

Allodi and Tovell 1989 – Allodi, Mary, and Rosemarie Tovell. *An Engraver's Pilgrimage: James Smillie in Quebec 1821–1830.* Toronto: Royal Ontario Museum, 1989.

Antique Silver Exhibitions **n.d.** – *Antique Silver Exhibitions: Including the Bradbury Loan Collection of Old Sheffield.* Montreal: Henry Birks and Sons, n.d.

Art au Canada **1962** – *L'art au Canada.* Bordeaux: Musée de Bordeaux, 1962 [exhibition catalogue].

Arts in French Canada **1959** – *The Arts in French Canada.* Vancouver: Vancouver Art Gallery, 1959 [exhibition catalogue].

Arts of French Canada **1946** – *The Arts of French Canada, 1613–1870.* Detroit: The Detroit Institute of Arts, 1946 [exhibition catalogue].

"Arts of Old Quebec" 1941 – "Arts of Old Quebec," typed list. Montreal: Art Association of Montreal, summer 1941.

Bailey 1982 – Bailey, Alfred G. "Babbitt, John." In *DCB.* Vol. 11 (1982), p. 39.

Barbeau 1935 – Barbeau, Marius. "Anciens orfèvres du Québec." *Transactions of the Royal Society of Canada,* 3rd series, 29:1 (1935), pp. 113–15.

Barbeau 1939a – "Nos anciens orfèvres." *Le Canada français,* no. 26 (June 1939), pp. 914–22.

Barbeau 1939b – "Nos anciens orfèvres." *Technique* 14:12 (Dec. 1939), pp. 666–68.

Barbeau 1939c – "Deux cents ans d'orfèvrerie chez-nous." *Transactions of the Royal Society of Canada,* 3rd series, 33:1 (1939), pp. 183–91.

Barbeau 1940 – "Indian Trade Silver." *Transactions of the Royal Society of Canada,* 3rd series, 34:2 (1940), pp. 27–41.

Barbeau 1941 – "Old Canadian Silver." *Canadian Geographical Journal* 22:1 (March 1941), pp. 150–62.

Barbeau 1957 – *Trésor des anciens jésuites.* Bulletin 153. Collection: Série anthropologique, 43. Ottawa: National Museums of Canada, 1957.

Bazin 1969 – Bazin, Jules, "Fézeret, René." In *DCB.* Vol. 2 (1969), p. 221.

Béchard 1885 – Béchard, A. *Histoire de la paroisse de Saint-Augustin.* Quebec City: The Parish, 1885.

Beuque 1962 – Beuque, Émile. *Dictionnaire des poinçons officiels français et étrangers, anciens et modernes de leur création (XVIᵉ siècle) à nos jours.* 2 vols. Paris: De Nobele, 1962.

Beuque and Frapsauce 1964 – Beuque, Émile, and M. Frapsauce. *Dictionnaire des poinçons de maîtres orfèvres français du XVIᵉ siècle à 1838.* Paris: De Nobele, 1964.

Bimbenet-Privat 1992 – Bimbenet-Privat, Michèle. *Les orfèvres parisiens de la Renaissance (1506–1620).* Paris: Commission des travaux historiques de la Ville de Paris, 1992.

Bimbenet-Privat 1995 – Ed. *Les orfèvres parisiens de la Renaissance: Trésors dispersés.* Paris: Centre culturel du Panthéon, 1995.

Birks 1925 – Birks, J. Earl. *The Romance of Silver Craft.* Toronto: Ryrie-Birks, 1925.

Birks Catalogue 1906 – *Catalogue 1906: The Gold and Silversmiths [and] Diamond Merchants.* Toronto: Henry Birks and Sons, 1906.

Birks Catalogue 1913 – *Catalogue 1913: Henry Birks and Sons Limited.* Montreal: Henry Birks and Sons, 1913.

Birks "Old Guard" **1944** – *Birks "Old Guard."* Montreal: Southam Press, 1944.

Bovey 1974 – Bovey, Patricia E. *The Development of Canadian Silver: A Winnipeg Centennial Exhibition*. Winnipeg Art Gallery, 3 April–30 Sept. 1974. Winnipeg: The Gallery, 1974 [exhibition catalogue].

Bradbury 1912 – Bradbury, Frederick. *History of Old Sheffield Plate*. London, England: Macmillan, 1912.

Brault and Bottineau 1959 – Brault, Solange, and Yves Bottineau. *L'orfèvrerie française du XVIIIᵉ siècle*. Series: L'œil du connaisseur. Paris: Presses universitaires de France, 1959.

Buhler and Hood 1970 – Buhler, Kathryn C., and Graham Hood. *American Silver: Garvan and Other Collections in the Yale University Art Gallery*. 2 vols. New Haven: Yale University Press, 1970.

***Canadian Handicrafts Guild* 1941** – *Canadian Handicrafts Guild Annual Report for the Year 1940*. Montreal: The Guild, 1941.

Carré 1928 – Carré, Louis. *Les poinçons de l'orfèvrerie française du quatorzième siècle jusqu'au début du dix-neuvième siècle*. Paris: F. de Nobele, 1928.

Carrier 1969 – Carrier, Maurice. "Baudry, *dit* Des Buttes, Guillaume." In *DCB*. Vol. 2 (1969), p. 48.

Cauchon and Juneau 1974a – Cauchon, Michel, and André Juneau. "Cotton, Michel." In *DCB*. Vol. 3 (1974), pp. 144, 145.

Cauchon and Juneau 1974b – "Deschevery, *dit* Maisonbasse, Jean-Baptiste." Ibid., pp. 181, 182.

Cauchon and Juneau 1974c – "Gadois, *dit* Mauger, Jacques." Ibid., pp. 232, 233.

Cauchon and Juneau 1974d – "Landron, Jean-François." Ibid., pp. 347, 348.

Cauchon and Juneau 1974e – "Pagé, *dit* Carcy, Jacques." Ibid., pp. 498, 499.

Cauchon and Juneau 1974f – "Paradis, Roland." Ibid., pp. 500, 501.

***Charles De Volpi* 1979** – *The Charles De Volpi Collection of Canadian Silver*. Toronto: Philips Ward-Price Limited, 1979 [catalogue for sale held 18 May 1979].

Chassay 1988 – Chassay, Sonia. "Signaÿ, Joseph." In *DCB*. Vol. 7 (1988), pp. 798–800.

***Collections* 1965** – *Collections of the Late Joseph H. Bauer, Esquire*. Toronto: Gardner Auctions Limited, 1965 [catalogue for auction held 15, 16, and 17 June 1965].

Cooke 1983 – Cooke, W. Martha E. *Canadian Collection of W.H. Coverdale: Paintings, Watercolours, and Drawings (Manoir Richelieu Collection)*. Ottawa: National Archives of Canada, 1983.

Corbeil 1954 – Corbeil, Gilles. "Collections et collectionneurs canadiens: Louis Carrier." *Arts et Pensées*, no. 16 (April 1954), pp. 115–18.

Culme 1977 – Culme, John. *Nineteenth-century Silver*. London, England: Country Life Books, 1977.

Culme 1994 – "Rundell, Bridge et Rundell et le commerce londonien de l'orfèvrerie." In *Orfèvrerie au XIXᵉ siècle* 1994, pp. 115–22.

De Pencier 1982 – De Pencier, Honor. "The John and Eustella Langdon Collection of Canadian Silver." *Rotunda* 15:1 (spring 1982), pp. 4–11.

Derome 1974a – Derome, Robert. "Delezenne: Les orfèvres, l'orfèvrerie (1740–90)." Master's thesis, Université de Montréal, Montreal, 1974.

Derome 1974b – *Les orfèvres de Nouvelle-France: Inventaire descriptif des sources*. Ottawa: National Gallery of Canada, 1974.

Derome 1975 – "Des poinçons de deux maîtres." *M24*. Montreal Museum of Fine Arts bulletin 6:4 (spring 1975), pp. 4–13.

Derome 1976 – "Delezenne, le maître de Ranvoyzé." *Vie des arts* 21:83 (summer 1976), pp. 56–58.

Derome 1979a – "Delezenne, Ignace-François." In *DCB*. Vol. 4 (1979), pp. 204–07.

Derome 1979b – "Picard, Louis-Alexandre." Ibid., pp. 628–30.

Derome 1979c – "Schindler, Joseph (Jonas)." Ibid., pp. 702, 703.

Derome 1979d – "Varin, *dit* La Pistole, Jacques." Ibid., pp. 748, 749.

Derome 1980a – "La collection Birks doit revenir au Québec." *Le Devoir* (Montreal), 23 Jan. 1980, p. 5.

Derome 1980b – "Comptes rendus: Quebec and Related Silver at the Detroit Institute of Arts…" *Annales d'histoire de l'art canadien* 5:1 (1980), pp. 69–74.

Derome 1981 – "Gérard Morisset et l'orfèvrerie." In *À la découverte du patrimoine avec Gérard Morisset*. Quebec City: Musée du Québec, 1981, pp. 205–20.

Derome 1983a – "Arnoldi, Michael." In *DCB*. Vol. 5 (1983), pp. 36, 37.

Derome 1983b – "Cruickshank, Robert." Ibid., pp. 217–19.

Derome 1983c – "Forton, Michel." Ibid., p. 329.

Derome 1987a – "Delezenne, Marie-Catherine." In *DCB*. Vol. 6 (1987), pp. 183–85.

Derome 1987b – "Ramsay Traquair: The History of Silver in Quebec and the McGill University Archives." In *Ramsay Traquair and His Successors: A Guide to the Archive*. Series: Canadian Architecture Collection. Montreal: McGill University, Blackader-Lauterman Library, 1987, pp. 78–105.

Derome 1992a – "The Church and Early Quebec Craft Traditions." In *A Treasury of Canadian Craft*. Inaugural exhibition, Canadian Craft Museum, Vancouver, 1 May–7 Sept. 1992, pp. 27–29 [exhibition catalogue].

Derome 1992b – "Orfèvrerie." *Questions de goût: Arts décoratifs et beaux-arts au McCord*. Montreal: McCord Museum of Canadian History, 1992, pp. 115–47.

Derome 1993 – "Les plus anciens outils et ateliers d'orfèvres au Québec." Edited by Christiane Eluère. In *Outils et ateliers d'orfèvres des temps anciens*. Series: Antiquités nationales, mémoire 2. Saint-Germain-en-Laye: Société des amis du Musée des Antiquités nationales et du château de Saint-Germain-en-Laye, avec le concours du ministère de la Culture, 1993, pp. 259–74.

Derome 1994a – "L'émigration des orfèvres français au Canada et ses conséquences sur l'orfèvrerie canadienne." In *Les orfèvres français sous l'Ancien Régime*, edited by Catherine Arminjon and Alain Erlande-Brandenburg. Publication of colloquium of the Association pour le développement de l'Inventaire général des Pays de la Loire, held in Nantes, 13 and 14 Oct. 1989. Nantes: The Association, 1994, pp. 105–08.

Derome 1994b – *L'acquisition de la Collection Henry Birks d'orfèvrerie canadienne par le Musée des beaux-arts du Canada en 1980*. Press kit prepared for the colloquium *Musée et collections: Impact des acquisitions massives* held at the Musée d'art contemporain, Montreal, 21 Oct. 1994. Montreal: Université du Québec à Montréal, 1994.

Derome and Henshaw 1987a – Derome, Robert, and Mary Henshaw. "Duval, Charles." In *DCB*. Vol. 6 (1987), pp. 230, 231.

Derome and Henshaw 1987b – "Rousseau, Dominique." Ibid., pp. 663–67.

Derome and Ménard 1983a – Derome, Robert, and José Ménard. "Ranvoyzé (Ranvoizé), François." In *DCB*. Vol. 5 (1983), pp. 707–10.

Derome and Ménard 1983b – "Roy, Narsise." Ibid., pp. 727, 728.

Derome and Ménard 1987 – "Marion, Salomon." In *DCB*. Vol. 6 (1987), pp. 487, 488.

Derome and Morgan 1983 – Derome, Robert, and Norma Morgan. "Huguet, *dit* Latour, Pierre," in *DCB*. Vol. 5 (1983), pp. 435–38.

Derome and Morgan 1985 – "Morand, Paul (Hypolithe)." In *DCB*. Vol. 8 (1985), pp. 637, 638.

Derome and Normand 1982 – Derome, Robert, and Sylvio Normand. "Lespérance (Rocheleau, *dit* Lespérance), Pierre." In *DCB*. Vol. 11 (1982), pp. 514–16.

Déziel 1951a – Déziel, Julien. "Gilles Beaugrand, orfèvre." *Arts et Pensées* 1:2 (March 1951), pp. 46–49.

Déziel 1951b – "Georges Delrue, joaillier." *Arts et Pensées* 1:6 (Nov. 1951), pp. 168–71.

Diderot 1964–66 – Diderot, Denis. *Encyclopédie, ou Dictionnaire raisonné des sciences: Recueil de planches sur les sciences, les arts libéraux, et les arts méchaniques, avec leur explication.* 11 vols. Paris: Cercle du livre précieux, 1964–66 (reprint of original).

Dion-Tenenbaum 1994 – "Jean-Charles Cahier et l'orfèvrerie religieuse." In *Orfèvrerie au XIXᵉ siècle* 1994, pp. 17–37.

Dubé 1969 – Dubé, Jean-Claude. *Claude-Thomas Dupuy: Intendant de la Nouvelle-France*. Montreal: Fides, 1969.

Dufrenne 1970 – Dufrenne, Mikel. "Style." In *Encyclopedia Universalis*. Vol. 15. Paris: Encyclopedia Universalis, 1968, pp. 463, 464.

Elwood 1983–84 – Elwood, Marie. "The Weldon Collection: Specimens of China Brought to the Colonies by the Early Settlers, Particularly the Loyalist." *Canadian Collector* 18:4 (July–Aug. 1983), pp. 26–29. The author comments further on the collection in the following issues: 18:5 (Sept.–Oct. 1983), pp. 20–27; 18:16 (Nov.–Dec. 1983), pp. 53–58; 19:1 (Jan.–Feb. 1984), pp. 36–42.

"Exhibition, 1932" 1933 – "Exhibition, 1932." *Canadian Handicrafts Guild Annual Report for the Year 1932*. Montreal: The Guild, 1933, pp. 20–23.

Exhibition of Canadian Handicrafts 1905 – *Exhibition of Canadian Handicrafts 1905*. Montreal, 14–28 Feb. 1905. Montreal: Montreal Branch Woman's Art Association, 1905 [exhibition catalogue].

Exposition rétrospective 1952 – *Exposition rétrospective de l'art au Canada français*. Quebec City: Musée de la province de Québec, 1952 [exhibition catalogue].

Exposition rétrospective des colonies françaises 1929 – *Exposition rétrospective des colonies françaises de l'Amérique du Nord*. Paris: Société d'éditions géographiques, maritimes et coloniales, 1929 [exhibition catalogue by Léo Leymarie].

Fabre-Surveyer 1940 – Fabre-Surveyer, E. "Une famille d'orfèvres." *Bulletin des recherches historiques* 46:10 (Oct. 1940), pp. 310–15.

Fifth Biennial Exhibition 1935 – *Fifth Biennial Exhibition of Architecture and Allied Arts*, section devoted to "Traditional Arts of French Canada," Art Gallery of Toronto, 4–(31?) January 1935. Organized by the Ontario Association of Architects, Toronto Chapter, with the collaboration of Marius Barbeau. Toronto: Art Gallery of Toronto, 1935 [exhibition catalogue].

Fine English 1988 – *Fine English and Continental Silver and Objects of Virtue*. New York: Christie's, 1988 [catalogue for auction held 25 Oct. 1988].

Fournier 1947 – Fournier, Thérèse. "Joaillier d'art." *La Revue Populaire*, Nov. 1947, p. 2.

Fox 1970 – Fox, Ross Allan C. *Quebec and Related Silver at the Detroit Institute of Arts*. Detroit: Wayne University Press, 1970.

Fox 1973 – "French Canadian Liturgical Silver." *Bulletin of Detroit Institute of Arts*, no. 52 (1973), pp. 97–105.

Fox 1985 – *Presentation Pieces and Trophies from the Henry Birks Collection of Canadian Silver.* Vancouver Museum (then Vancouver Centennial Museum), 1 March–30 April 1984; Centre culturel du Bas-Saint-Laurent, Rivière-du-Loup, Quebec, 1–30 June 1984; Moncton Museum, 1 Sept.–31 Oct. 1984; Northern Life Museum, Fort Smith, Northwest Territories, 1–31 Dec. 1984; Nickel Arts Museum, Calgary, 15 Jan.–15 Feb. 1985; Rodman Hall Arts Centre, St Catharines, 3–31 March 1985; Art Gallery of Peterborough, 15 April–15 May 1985; Art Gallery of Algoma, Sault Ste Marie, 1–30 June 1985. Ottawa: National Gallery of Canada, 1985 [exhibition catalogue].

Fox 1990 – "Hendery, Robert." In *DCB.* Vol. 12 (1990), pp. 424, 425.

François Ranvoyzé **1968** – *François Ranvoyzé, orfèvre (1739–1819).* Quebec City: Musée du Québec, 1968 [exhibition catalogue].

Frederickson and Gibb 1980 – Frederickson, N. Jaye, and Sandra Gibb. *The Covenance Chain: Indian Ceremonial and Trade Silver.* Ottawa: Canadian Museum of Civilization (then National Museum of Man) / National Museums of Canada, 1980.

French in America **1951** – *The French in America.* Detroit: The Detroit Institute of Arts, 1951 [exhibition catalogue].

Gagné and Asselin 1967 – Gagné, Lucien, and Jean-Pierre Asselin. *Sainte-Anne de Beaupré: Trois cents ans de pèlerinage.* Sainte-Anne de Beaupré, Quebec: The Basilica, 1967.

Gauvreau 1940a – Gauvreau, Jean-Marie, "L'École du Meuble renaît." *Technique* 15:8 (Oct. 1940), pp. 527–32.

Gauvreau 1940b – *Artisans du Québec.* Trois-Rivières: Les Éditions du Bien public, 1940.

George 1946 – George, A. Robert. *The House of Birks: A History of Henry Birks and Sons.* Montreal: Henry Birks and Sons, 1946.

Giguère 1972 – Giguère, G.E. "L'orfèvre François Ranvoyzé." *Vidéo-Presse* 1:7 (April 1972), pp. 40–42.

Giguère 1980 – "Les institutions qui nous ont faits: La collection Birks." Ibid. 10:1 (Sept. 1980), pp. 40, 41.

Gilbey 1910 – Gilbey, Walter. *Racing Cups 1559–1850.* London, England: Vinton and Co., 1910.

Gooding 1962 – Gooding, S. James. *The Canadian Gunsmiths 1608–1900.* West Hill, Toronto: Museum Restoration Service, 1962.

Gosselin 1896 – Gosselin, Amédée. *Henri de Bernières, premier curé de Québec.* Évreux, France, 1896.

Grand Héritage **1984** – *Le Grand Héritage: L'Église catholique et les arts au Québec.* Quebec City: Gouvernement du Québec, 1984 [exhibition catalogue].

Green 1994 – Green, J. Paul. "Muir, Alexander." In *DCB.* Vol. 13 (1994), pp. 745, 746.

Greening 1962 – Greening, W.E. "Loretteville and the Treasure of the Jesuits." *Canadian Geographical Journal* 65:3 (Sept. 1962), pp. 90–94.

Greening 1966 – "Silversmiths of French Canada." *The Connoisseur* 162:653 (July 1966), pp. 213–17.

Greenwood 1978 – Greenwood, Michael. *Historic Canadian Silver from the Henry Birks Collection.* Art Gallery of York University, Toronto, 9 Sept.–10 Oct. 1978; Henry Birks store, Eaton Centre, Toronto, 24 Oct.–11 Nov. 1978. Toronto: The Gallery, 1978 [exhibition catalogue].

Grimwade 1985 – Grimwade, Arthur. "New Light on Canadian Treasure: The Royal Communion Service of Quebec." *Country Life*, no. 177 (31 Jan. 1985), pp. 268–73.

Grimwade 1990 – *London Goldsmiths 1637–1837: Their Marks and Lives from the Original Registers at Goldsmiths' Hall and Other Sources.* London, England: Faber and Faber, 1990.

Gruber 1982 – Gruber, Alain. *L'argenterie de maison du XVIe au XIXe siècle.* Fribourg: Office du Livre, 1982.

Gruber 1992a – Ed. *L'art décoratif en Europe: Classique et baroque.* Paris: Citadelles and Mazenod, 1992.

Gruber 1992b – Ed. *L'art décoratif en Europe: Du néoclassicisme à l'Art Déco.* Ibid.

Hare et al. 1987 – Hare, John, Marc Lafrance, and David-Thiery Rudell. *Histoire de la ville de Québec 1608–1871.* Montreal: Boréal / Canadian Museum of Civilization, 1987.

Helft 1968 – Helft, Jacques. *Le poinçon des provinces françaises.* Paris: De Nobele, 1968.

Helft 1980 – *Nouveaux poinçons.* Following from *Recherches techniques et historiques sur l'orfèvrerie sous l'Ancien Régime.* Paris: Berger-Levrault, 1980.

Hommage à Jean Palardy **1984** – *Hommage à Jean Palardy.* Montreal: Musée d'art de Saint-Laurent, 1984.

Hubbard 1983 – Hubbard, Robert Hamilton. "Ramage, John." In *DCB.* Vol. 5 (1983), pp. 704–06.

Ignatieff 1981 – Ignatieff, Helena. "Canadian Presentation Pieces and Awards of Merit." *Canadian Collector* 16:6 (Nov.–Dec. 1981), pp. 40–42.

Iguarta 1974 – Iguarta, José. "Terroux, Jacques." In *DCB.* Vol. 3 (1974), p. 620.

Jones 1913 – Jones, E. Alfred. *The Old Silver of American Churches.* Letchworth, England: Privately printed for the National Society of Colonial Dames of America, by Arden Press, 1913.

Jones 1918 – "Old Church Silver in Canada." *Transactions of the Royal Society of Canada,* 3rd series, 12:2 (1918), p. 135.

Juneau 1968 – Juneau, André. "Orfèvrerie indienne." *Bulletin du Musée du Québec,* no. 9 (Aug. 1968), pp. 1–5.

Juneau 1969 – "Soullard, Jean." In *DCB.* Vol. 2 (1969), p. 612.

Karel 1992 – Karel, David. *Dictionnaire des artistes de langue française en Amérique du Nord.* Quebec City: Presses de l'Université Laval / Musée du Québec, 1992.

Kauffman 1969 – Kauffman, Henry J. *The Colonial Silversmith: His Technique and His Products.* New York: Galahad Books, 1969.

L'Allier 1977 – L'Allier, Pierre. *Héritage vivant de l'orfèvrerie: Vingt pièces de la collection du Musée du Québec.* Quebec City: Musée du Québec, 1977 [exhibition catalogue].

Lanel 1949 – Lanel, Luc. *L'orfèvrerie.* Series: Que sais-je?, no. 131. Paris: Presses universitaires de France, 1949.

Langdon 1938 – Langdon, John Emerson. "Early Silversmiths and Canadian Currency." *The Canadian Banker* 45:2 (Jan. 1938), pp. 165–69.

Langdon 1942 – "Early Canadian Silver." *Antiques* 41:5 (May 1942), pp. 300–02.

Langdon 1960 – *Canadian Silversmiths and Their Marks, 1667–1867.* Lunenburg, Vermont: Privately printed, 1960.

Langdon 1966 – *Canadian Silversmiths, 1700–1900.* Toronto: Stinehour Press, 1966.

Langdon 1968 – *Guide to Marks on Early Canadian Silver.* Toronto: Ryerson Press, 1968.

Langdon 1969a – "Levasseur, Michel." In *DCB.* Vol. 2 (1969), p. 430.

Langdon 1969b – "Silversmithing in Canada during the French Colonial Period." In *Fourteenth Annual Winterthur Conference 1968.* Winterthur, Delaware: Henry Francis du Pont Winterthur Museum, 1969, pp. 47–64.

Langdon 1974 – "Lambert, *dit* Saint-Paul, Paul." In *DCB.* Vol. 3 (1974), pp. 346, 347.

Lindsay 1900 – Lindsay, Lionel Saint-George. *Notre-Dame de la Jeune-Lorette en la Nouvelle-France.* Montreal: La compagnie de publication de la *Revue Canadienne,* 1900.

Lyman 1943 – Lyman, Elisha. *Genealogy of the Lyman Family in Canada*. Montreal: The Beaver Hall Press, 1943.

Mabille 1984 – Mabille, Gérard. *Orfèvrerie française des XVIᵉ, XVIIᵉ, XVIIIᵉ siècles: Catalogue raisonné des collections du Musée des arts décoratifs et du Musée Nissim de Camondo*. Paris: Flammarion / Musée des arts décoratifs, c. 1984.

Mackay 1972 – Mackay, Donald C. "Goldsmiths and Silversmiths." *Canadian Antiques Collector* 7:1 (Jan. 1972), pp. 22–26.

Mackay 1973 – *Silversmiths and Related Craftsmen of the Atlantic Provinces*. Halifax: Petheric Press, 1973.

MacLeod 1979 – MacLeod, Kenneth O. *The First Century: The Story of a Canadian Company – Henry Birks and Sons, 1879–1979*. Montreal: Privately published, 1979.

Massicotte 1917 – Massicotte, Édouard-Zotique. "La Saint-Éloi et la corporation des armuriers à Montréal au 17ᵉ siècle." *Bulletin des recherches historiques* 23:10 (Oct. 1917), pp. 343–46.

Massicotte 1924 – "Café, thé et chocolat en la Nouvelle-France." Ibid. 30:6 (June 1924), p. 199.

Massicotte 1929 – "La coutellerie de table et de traite sous le régime français." Ibid. 35:5 (May 1929), pp. 263–67.

Massicotte 1930 – "Orfèvres et bijoutiers du régime français." Ibid. 36:1 (Jan. 1930), pp. 30–32.

Massicotte 1931 – "Fondeurs de cuillers." Ibid. 37:8 (Aug. 1931), pp. 518–21.

Massicotte 1938 – "Bagues, anneaux, alliances." Ibid. 44:9 (Sept. 1938), pp. 279–81.

Massicotte 1940a – "L'argentier Huguet-Latour." Ibid. 46:9 (Sept. 1940), pp. 353–56.

Massicotte 1940b – "Deux orfèvres d'autrefois (Jean Villain et Samuel Payne)." Ibid. 46:12 (Dec. 1940), pp. 353–56.

Massicotte 1943a – "Les tabatières de nos grands-parents." Ibid. 49:1 (Jan. 1943), pp. 10–13.

Massicotte 1943b – "Dominique Rousseau, maître orfèvre et négociant en pelleteries." Ibid. 49:11 (Nov. 1943), pp. 342–48.

Massicotte and Roy 1918 – Massicotte, Édouard-Zotique, and Régis Roy. *Armorial du Canada français*. Montreal: Beauchemin, 1918.

Maurault 1930 – Maurault, Olivier. *Oka: Les vicissitudes d'une mission sauvage*. Reprinted in part from *Revue trimestrielle canadienne*, June 1930. Montreal: *Le Devoir*, 1930.

Maurault 1947 – "Les trésors d'une église de campagne." *Transactions of the Royal Society of Canada*, 3rd series, 41:1 (1947), pp. 55–63.

McClinton 1968 – McClinton, Katharine Morrison. *Collecting American Nineteenth-century Silver*. New York: Charles Scribner's Sons, 1968.

McNab 1981 – McNab, Jessie. *Silver*. Series: The Smithsonian Illustrated Library of Antiques. New York: Cooper-Hewitt Museum of Decorative Arts and Design, Smithsonian Institution, 1981.

Montreal Gazette **1851** – *Montreal Gazette*, 28 July 1851, p. 2.

Montreal Gazette **1859** – *Montreal Gazette*, 30 July 1859, p. 2.

Montreal Herald **1834** – *Montreal Herald*, 22 Sept. 1834, p. 2.

Montreal Transcript **1851** – *Montreal Transcript*, 2 Aug. 1851, p. 2.

Moogk 1969 – Moogk, Peter. "Payne, Samuel." In *DCB*. Vol. 2 (1969), pp. 513, 514.

Morisset 1941 – Morisset, Gérard. *Coup d'œil sur les arts en Nouvelle-France*. Quebec City: [Charrier et Dugal], 1941.

Morisset 1942a – *Exposition de photographies d'argenteries québécoise: François Ranvoyzé (Québec 1739–Québec 1819)*. École des beaux-arts de Québec, Quebec City, 1942; Montreal, 1942; Institut français, New York, 1942. Quebec City: Secrétariat de la Province, 1942 [exhibition catalogue].

Morisset 1942b – *François Ranvoyzé*. Collection: Champlain. Quebec City: Médium, 1942.

Morisset 1943a – *Évolution d'une pièce d'argenterie*. Ibid., 1943.

Morisset 1943b – *Les églises et le trésor de Varennes*. Ibid.

Morisset 1945a – "L'orfèvre François Chambellan." *Bulletin des recherches historiques* 51:1–2 (Jan.–Feb. 1945), pp. 31–35.

Morisset 1945b – "L'instrument de paix." *Transactions of the Royal Society of Canada*, 3rd series, 39:1 (1945), pp. 143–61.

Morisset 1945c – *Paul Lambert*, dit *Saint-Paul*. Collection: Champlain. Quebec City and Montreal: Médium, 1945.

Morisset 1947a – "L'orfèvrerie canadienne." *Technique* 22:3 (March 1947), pp. 83–88.

Morisset 1947b – "Nos orfèvres canadiens: Pierre Lespérance." Ibid. 22:4 (April 1947), pp. 201–09.

Morisset 1947c – "La tasse à quêter." *Transactions of the Royal Society of Canada*, 3rd series, 41:1 (May 1947), pp. 63–68.

Morisset 1947d – "Un quart d'heure chez Ranvoyzé." *La Petite Revue* 16:5 (May 1947), pp. 3–5, 34.

Morisset 1947e – "L'orfèvre Michel Levasseur." *Revue de l'Université d'Ottawa*, vol. 17 (1947), pp. 339–49.

Morisset 1948 – "Les arts sous le régime français." *Canadian Historical Association Report*. Ottawa: The Association, 1948, pp. 23–27.

Morisset 1949 – "Le trésor de la mission d'Oka." *La Patrie* (Montreal), 13 Nov. 1949, p. 18.

Morisset 1950a – "L'orfèvre Paul Lambert, *dit* Saint-Paul." Ibid., 1 Jan. 1950, pp. 14, 38.

Morisset 1950b – "Un cordonnier orfèvre: Michel Cotton." Ibid., 26 Feb. 1950, pp. 18, 26.

Morisset 1950c – "Les vases d'or de l'église de L'Islet." Ibid., 12 March 1950, pp. 18, 42.

Morisset 1950d – "L'orfèvre Louis-Alexandre Picard." Ibid., 30 April 1950, pp. 37, 38.

Morisset 1950e – "L'orfèvre François Sasseville." Ibid., 4 June 1950, pp. 26, 35.

Morisset 1950f – "Un perruquier orfèvre." Ibid., 2 July 1950, pp. 28–30.

Morisset 1950g – "L'orfèvrerie française au Canada." Ibid., 22 Oct. 1950, pp. 26, 27, 55.

Morisset 1950h – "L'orfèvre Roland Paradis." Ibid., 26 Nov. 1950, pp. 26, 31.

Morisset 1950i – "Jacques Pagé, *dit* Quercy." *Technique* 25:9 (Nov. 1950), pp. 589–600.

Morisset 1954a – "L'orfèvre Paul Morand 1784–1854." *Transactions of the Royal Society of Canada*, 3rd series, 48:1 (June 1954), pp. 29–36.

Morisset 1954b – "L'orfèvrerie canadienne." *La Revue française* 6:59 (Aug. 1954), pp. 60–64.

Morisset 1954c – "L'orfèvre Roland Paradis." *Technique* 29:7 (Sept. 1954), pp. 437–42.

Morisset 1955a – "Les vases d'or de l'église de L'Islet." Ibid. 30:4 (April 1955), pp. 227–31.

Morisset 1955b – "L'orfèvre François Sasseville." *Transactions of the Royal Society of Canada*, 3rd series, 49:1 (June 1955), pp. 51–54.

Morisset 1956a – "Louis-Nicolas Gaudin, *dit* Lapoterie." *Bulletin des recherches historiques* 62:1 (Jan.–March 1956), pp. 157, 158.

Morisset 1956b – "Nicolas Gaudin, *dit* Lapoterie." Ibid. 62:3 (July–Sept. 1956), pp. 47–53.

Morisset 1966a – "Olivier, *dit* le Picard, Marc-Antoine." In *DCB*. Vol. 1 (1966), p. 524.

Morisset 1966b – "Villain, Jean-Baptiste." Ibid., p. 679.

Morisset 1968 – "Notre orfèvrerie au XVIIIᵉ siècle." *Forces*, no. 5 (spring–summer 1968), pp. 14–17.

Morisset 1980 – *Le Cap-Santé: Ses églises, son trésor*. Montreal: Montreal Museum of Fine Arts, 1980. Reprint of original, with commentaries by Christiane Beauregard, Robert Derome, Laurier Lacroix, Luc Noppen, and Michel Gaumond.

Morning Chronicle **1851** – *Morning Chronicle* (Quebec City), 30 July 1851, p. 2.

Musée du Québec **1983** – *Le Musée du Québec: 500 œuvres choisies*. Quebec City: Gouvernement du Québec, 1983 [exhibition catalogue].

Nanavati 1977 – Nanavati, Tara Douglas. "Nineteenth-century Canadian Presentation Silver." Master's thesis, University of Toronto, 1977.

Nanavati c. 1978 – *A Sterling Past: The Silversmiths of Canada – An Exhibition of Antique Canadian Silver from the Henry Birks Collection*. Royal British Columbia Museum, Victoria, Sept. 1978–15 Jan. 1979; Glenbow-Alberta Institute, Calgary; Provincial Museum of Alberta, Edmonton; Vancouver Museum (formerly Vancouver Centennial Museum). Victoria: The Museum, c. 1978 [exhibition catalogue].

Newfoundland Historic Trust **1971** – *The Newfoundland Historic Trust Antiques Exhibition; The Henry Birks Collection of Canadian Silver; Newfoundland Pine Furniture; The Newfoundland and Labrador Sketches of Rev. W. Grey*. Arts and Culture Centre, St John's, Newfoundland, under the patronage of the Extension Service, Memorial University, 3 June–3 Aug. 1971. St John's: The Centre, 1971 [exhibition catalogue].

Newman 1987 – Newman, Harold. *An Illustrated Dictionary of Silverware*. New York: Thames and Hudson, 1987.

Nocq 1926 – Nocq, Henry. *Le poinçon de Paris*. 5 vols. Paris: H. Floury, 1926–31.

Noppen 1990 – Noppen, Luc. "Le mobilier traditionnel et le mobilier québécois des XIXᵉ et XXᵉ siècle." In *Objets de civilisation*. Quebec City: Musée de la Civilisation / Éditions Broquet, 1990, pp. 39–60.

Noppen 1991 – "De l'art d'habiter." *Continuité*, no. 51 (fall 1991), pp. 15–18.

Noppen and Villeneuve 1984 – Noppen, Luc, and René Villeneuve. *Le Trésor du Grand Siècle*. Quebec City: Musée du Québec, 1984 [exhibition catalogue].

Normand 1983 – Normand, Sylvio. "Hanna, James G." In *DCB*. Vol. 5 (1983), pp. 406, 407.

Notre-Dame Museum **1943** – *Notre-Dame Museum: Illustrated Catalogue*. 3rd ed. Montreal: The Museum, 1943.

Orfèvrerie au XIXᵉ siècle **1994** – *L'orfèvrerie au XIXᵉ siècle*. Edited by Catherine Arminjon. Publication of international colloquium held at the Galeries nationales du Grand Palais, Paris, 12 and 13 Dec. 1991. Paris: La Documentation française, 1994.

Pichette 1976 – Pichette, Robert. "Deux blasons canadien identifié." *Heraldry in Canada* 10:1 (March 1976), pp. 5–10.

Pichette and Vachon 1976 – Pichette, Robert A., and Auguste Vachon. *An Exhibition of Armorial Silver from the Henry Birks Collection of Canadian Silver*. National Archives of Canada, Ottawa, Oct. 1976. Ottawa: The Heraldry Society of Canada, 1976 [exhibition catalogue].

Radio-Collège **1941** – *Radio-Collège: Programme-horaire de la saison 1941–1942*. Montreal?: Société Radio-Canada, 1941?

Renzius 1945 – Renzius, Rudy. *Hammered Silver Flatware*. Toronto: Macmillan, 1945.

Roy 1930 – Roy, Antoine. *Les lettres, les sciences et les arts au Canada sous le Régime français: Essai de contribution à l'histoire de la civilisation canadienne*. Paris: Jouve, 1930.

Roy 1933 – Roy, Pierre-Georges. *Fils de Québec*. 4th series. Lévis, Quebec: Privately published, 1933.

Ryrie Bros 1929 – *Ryrie Bros Ltd, Toronto: Diamond Merchants, Jewellers, Silversmiths*. Toronto: Ryrie-Birks, 1929 [sales catalogue].

Schapiro 1994 – Schapiro, Meyer. *Theory and Philosophy of Art: Style, Artist, and Society*. New York: George Braziller, 1994.

Schwartz 1961 – Schwartz, Herbert J. "Les orfèvres de la Nouvelle-France." *Vie des arts*, no. 24 (autumn–winter 1961), pp. 39–45.

Schwartz 1963 – "L'ancienne splendeur de Caughnawaga." *Vie des arts*, no. 33 (winter 1963), pp. 56–59.

Silver Thread 1970 – *The Silver Thread through Canadian History: The Henry Birks Collection of Canadian Silver*. Montreal: Canadian Industries Limited (La Maison Del Vecchio) 1970 [exhibition catalogue].

Spalding 1979 – Spalding, Jeffrey J. *Silversmithing in Canadian History*. Calgary: Glenbow-Alberta Institute, c. 1979.

Thibault 1973 – Thibault, Claude. *Trésors des communautés réligieuses de la Ville de Québec*. Quebec City: Department of Cultural Affairs / Éditeur officiel du Québec, 1973.

Thomson 1967 – Thomson, A.S. "Canadian Silversmiths." *Canadian Collector* 2:2 (Feb. 1967), pp. 12, 13.

Thuilé 1959 – Thuilé, Jean. "Un souvenir canadien du maréchal Montcalm." *Revue de la Xᵉ Région économique*, April 1959, pp. 3, 4.

Traquair 1938 – Traquair, Ramsay. "Montreal and Indian Trade Silver." *The Canadian Historical Review* 19:1 (March 1938), pp. 1–8.

Traquair 1940 – *The Old Silver of Quebec*. Toronto: Macmillan, 1940.

Trudel 1968a – Trudel, Jean R. "À l'enseigne des orfèvres du Québec." *Culture vivante*, no. 10 (Aug. 1968), pp. 9–13.

Trudel 1968b – "Un maître orfèvre du Québec, François Ranvoyzé (1739–1819)." *Vie des arts*, no. 51 (summer 1968), pp. 63–65.

Trudel 1969a – "A New Light on Ranvoyzé." *Canadian Collector* 4:1 (Jan. 1969), p. 11.

Trudel 1969b – *Profil de la sculpture québécoise, XVIIᵉ–XIXᵉ siècles*. Quebec City: Musée du Québec, 1969 [exhibition catalogue].

Trudel 1972 – "Early Canadian Silver." *Canadian Antiques Collector* 7:2 (March–April 1972), pp. 20, 21.

Trudel 1973a – "L'orfèvrerie en Nouvelle-France." *Vie des arts* 18:73 (winter 1973–74), pp. 45–49.

Trudel 1973b – "Étude sur une statue en argent de Salomon Marion." *Bulletin: The National Gallery of Canada, Ottawa*, no. 21 (1973), pp. 3–19 (English summary by the author, p. 34).

Trudel 1974a – "La mission de l'argenterie française aux 17ᵉ et 18ᵉ siècles mieux comprise par l'étude de quelques pièces rares récemment recensées en Nouvelle-France." *Connaissance des arts*, no. 264 (Feb. 1974), pp. 58–63.

Trudel 1974b – *Silver in New France*. Ottawa: National Gallery of Canada, 1974 [exhibition catalogue].

Trudel 1976 – "Sasseville, François." In *DCB*. Vol. 9 (1976), pp. 701, 702.

Trudel 1984 – "Trésors de la fabrique Saint-Augustin." In *Grand Héritage* 1984.

Trudel et al. 1968 – Trudel, Jean R., Georges Massey, and André Juneau. *François Ranvoyzé, orfèvre, 1739–1819*. Quebec City: Ministère des Affaires culturelles / Musée du Québec, 1968 [exhibition catalogue].

Turner 1994 – Turner, Eric. "Les substituts de l'argent au XVIIIᵉ et XIXᵉ siècles." In *Orfèvrerie au XIXᵉ siècle* 1994, pp. 137–43.

"Two Pieces" 1919 – "Two Pieces of Canadian Ecclesiastical Silver." *The Burlington Magazine* 34:191 (Feb. 1919), pp. 74, 75.

Vallée 1937 – Vallée, Arthur. *Notes brèves sur quelques documents et pièces du trésor historique de l'Hôtel-Dieu de Kebec.* 2nd ed. Quebec City: [Hôtel-Dieu], 1937.

Vallières 1984 – Vallières, Nicole. *Art et techniques de l'orfèvrerie aux XVIIIᵉ et XIXᵉ siècles.* Montreal: Musée d'art de Saint-Laurent, 1984 [exhibition catalogue].

Venable 1996 – Venable, Charles L. *Silver in America 1840–1940: A Century of Splendor.* Dallas: Dallas Museum of Art, 1996 [exhibition catalogue].

Villeneuve 1983 – Villeneuve, René. "L'orfèvrerie ancienne." In *Musée du Québec* 1983, pp. 307–42.

Villeneuve 1987 – "Orkney, James." In *DCB*. Vol. 6 (1987), pp. 556, 557.

Villeneuve 1988a – "English Influences on Quebec Silver." *The Antique Collector* 59:10 (Oct. 1988), pp. 58–63.

Villeneuve 1988b – "Amiot, Laurent." In *DCB*. Vol. 7 (1988), pp. 16–18.

Villeneuve 1994 – "Lafrance, Ambroise." In *DCB*. Vol. 13 (1994), pp. 563, 564.

Villeneuve 1997 – *Baroque to Neo-Classical: Sculpture in Quebec.* Ottawa: National Gallery of Canada, 1997.

Ward et al. 1980 – Ward, Gerald W.R., Patricia E. Kane, and Helen A. Cooper. *Francis P. Garvan, Collector.* New Haven: Yale University Art Gallery, 1980.

Wardle 1963 – Wardle, Patricia. *Victorian Silver and Silver Plate.* London, England: Herbert Jenkins, 1963.

Wenham 1927 – Wenham, Edward. "Early Silversmiths in Canada." *Canadian Homes and Gardens* 4:7 (July 1927), p. 36.

Wenham 1929 – "Canada's Early Silversmiths." *The Spur*, June 1929, pp. 96, 114.

William Hugh Coverdale **1980** – *William Hugh Coverdale, collectionneur.* La Malbaie, Quebec: Musée régional Laure Conan, 1980.

Wrong 1926 – Wrong, George M. *A Canadian Manor and Its Seigneurs.* Toronto: Macmillan, 1926.

INDEX OF SILVER

Includes illustrated silver and objects, and silver from the collection of the National Gallery that is referenced in the text.